30-x-08

TROOP
LEADER

TROOP LEADER

A TANK COMMANDER'S STORY

Bill Bellamy

BILL BELLAMY

FOREWORD BY
RICHARD HOLMES

SUTTON PUBLISHING

First published in the United Kingdom in 2005 by
Sutton Publishing Limited

Paperback edition first published in 2007

Reprinted in 2007 by Sutton Publishing,
an imprint of NPI Media Group Limited
Cirencester Road · Chalford · Stroud · Gloucestershire · GL6 8PE

British Library Cataloguing in Publication Data
A catalogue record for this book is available from the British
Library.

ISBN 978-0-7509-4534-9

Typeset in 11/13 pt Photina MT.
Typesetting and origination by
Sutton Publishing Limited.
Printed and bound in England.

Contents

List of Plates and Maps

Plates

LIST OF PLATES AND MAPS

Maps and Sketches (as drawn by the author at that time)

Foreword

'I have always enjoyed writing,' observes Bill Bellamy at
the start of this book, and it shows in the pages that
follow. His account of life in the 8th King's Royal Irish
Hussars is a masterpiece of military history in the minor
key. He is not preoccupied with big battles or great generals,
but with the day-to-day minutiae of a tank regiment in
North-West Europe in 1944–5. It is an affectionate snapshot
of the army of sixty years ago, and also a penetrating
insight into the age-old alchemy that binds men together in
the claustrophobic world of the tank troop and armoured
vehicle crew.

The recurrent themes, never laboured but always there,
are decency and duty. Bill Bellamy went from public school
to the army as a private soldier at the age of eighteen. Once
trained, he went to Sandhurst, where he learnt 'very little of
technical or tactical value', but imbibed a 'philosophy of
duty' which put others first. He just managed to join his
regiment in North Africa before it came back to England for
D-Day. After landing on Gold Beach he spent the first weeks
of the campaign responsible for his squadron's transport,
leading trucks full of fuel and ammunition forward at night
through the bocage south of Bayeux.

Soon given a troop of Cromwell tanks to command, he fell
under the spell of his squadron leader, 'a demi-god, totally
unflappable and always prepared to listen', and the
inevitable intimacies of life inside a steel hull brought him
close to the men he commanded. Death plucked away his
comrades, and the rough little realities of war made their

mark. Dust, funnelled in through a tank's few apertures, gave crewmen conjunctivitis; piercing sunlight and frequent use of binoculars brought temporary blindness; and the half-crushed body of a German at a crossroads gave a sense of 'revulsion and sacrilege . . .'.

Having been involved in Operation Goodwood and the fighting around Mont Pinçon, Bill Bellamy took part in the great sweep into Belgium, which ended in wintry stalemate on the Dutch border. Although worldly wise in many ways, he remained naïve in others. News of his Military Cross was followed by a party, but when his landlady came and sat on his bed he did not quite realise that she was 'offering to complete my evening in the traditional way!' And he no longer looked the smart cavalry officer: 'I wore pyjamas under my underclothes, a thick shirt and sweater, corduroy trousers and that marvellous fur-collared American jacket.' His mother was killed by one of the first V2 rockets to hit London, but hatred for the Germans was soon blunted by the sight of the ruins of Hamburg and, after the war had ended, by the suffering of the population of Berlin, where 'life was cheap'.

This memoir gives affectionate sketches of the characters that no regiment, then or now, can be complete without, like the decorated trooper who greeted him with the irreverent exclamation: 'Cor, f——g schoolboys now,' the debonair captain with 'sleek black hair well buttered back,' and the 'solid and capable' Bill Pritchard, doyen of troop sergeants. It speaks volumes about the British army at the end of a long war – and about British soldiers across so much of history.

Richard Holmes

Preface

I have always enjoyed writing. As a child, and later at boarding school, this took the form of essays and poetry. When I went into the Army at the end of 1941, I continued this practice and wrote accounts of my experiences almost as they happened, a habit which continues to this day. These, together with notes, maps and photographs, were tucked away in a box which I retained when Ann and I were married in 1950. For the first forty years or so, I didn't want to think about the war, but some time after I had retired the box came out of the attic and down to my office.

My wife suggested that I should put the material into book form and give copies to our family, both as a record of my early years in the 8th King's Royal Irish Hussars and of my participation in the campaign that took place in north-west Europe in 1944–5. I did so, and produced a few copies of a book which I called 'Schoolboy's War' on my computer. In the event it proved an interesting exercise. It recalled, in a very special way, a most exciting period of my life and made me realise how fortunate I was to have survived, when so many of my friends perished. I was very lucky.

It is by its nature a very personal account, perhaps rather naïve, but then I was quite young. Apart from correcting several minor mistakes and expanding one or two points for the sake of clarity, the book is exactly as written shortly after the events which it describes took place.

I owe special thanks to my wife, who was a constant source of encouragement; to Alan Howard, who served

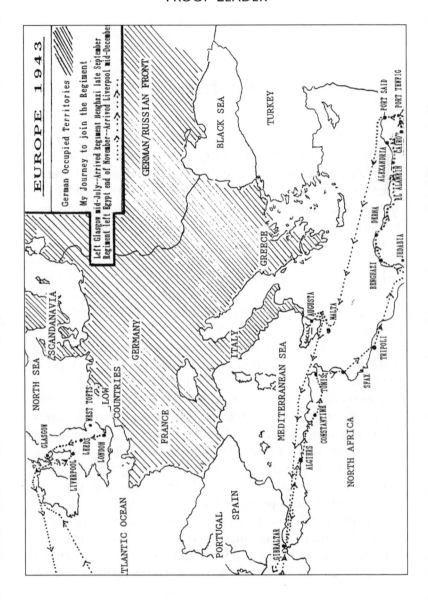

EUROPE 1943

German Occupied Territories

My Journey to join the Regiment

Left Glasgow mid-July--Arrived Regiment Benghazi late September
Regiment left Egypt end of November--Arrived Liverpool mid-December

alongside me as my Troop Corporal and was a valuable source of information; to Major Bill Best, our LAD officer, for the free use of his library of war photographs. It is a great shame that none of these is alive now to see it published.

I am also deeply grateful to Professor Richard Holmes who has not only been most encouraging but also has written the Foreword, and to the staff at Sutton Publishing who have been such a pleasure to work with.

Bill Bellamy

ONE

From School to Regiment

'Stick to your original ambition, my boy,' said my father, 'join the Royal Navy! Make a career of it.' He was visiting me at my school, Blackfriars, Laxton, making me the envy of my peers. He was an heroic figure to us, having recently escaped from France via Brest. At that time he was camp commandant of 1st Armoured Division and was completing his embarkation leave before departing once more, this time for Egypt. I saw him positively blossom in wartime. He had served in France in 1918, loved all that was military, and had rejoined the Army in 1938. I longed to follow his example and 'join up'. My constant prayer was that the war would not finish before I was old enough to fight.

My final term at Blackfriars was a busy one, I was head prefect, captain of the rugby team, patrol leader of the Owl Patrol, and a lance corporal in the Wakerley and Barrowden Home Guard. At the same time I was, theoretically, attempting to get enough passes in the Higher Certificate to allow me to read history at Peterhouse. I found it very difficult to concentrate on anything except the war, which at this time was going very badly for the Allies. My mother and grandmother lived together in Shepherds Bush, West London. The bombing was intensifying and there were concerns over their safety. My mother, a dress designer, had been given war work and appointed to assist in the distribution of meat to the ships in the Thames. Her places of work were Smithfield

Market and the London docks, both being the most heavily bombed areas. I took to going to Mass at 6 every morning, followed by a 4-mile run and a cold shower. This was intended to make me fit both spiritually and physically.

In October 1941, my father left for the Middle East with 1st Armoured Division. On hearing this I reported to the recruiting office in Northampton and volunteered for the RAF. The newspapers at that time were full of heartwarming stories about heroic pilots, and I was impatient to become one of them. In the event, it appeared that everyone else had the same desire and there were no vacancies. I was very downcast, but remembering my father's words, went along to the Royal Navy stand. At this stage of the war one still had, to some degree anyway, the opportunity to choose in which arm of the services one wished to serve. For some inexplicable reason, when I got there I wasn't attracted to the Royal Navy, and wandered on past the other recruiting stands. One, with pictures of the tanks in the Desert War, caught my eye. I hesitated there, and immediately a very smart sergeant buttonholed me and asked me if I was interested in the Royal Armoured Corps. I told him about my father and asked if I would be allowed to join him in the 1st Armoured Division. 'Very easy, laddie,' said the sergeant, 'as you have a father in the tanks [which he wasn't] you can go straight to the Armoured Training Regiment and in six months you'll be able to go out to Egypt.' On that promise, forgetting about the Royal Navy, I signed up.

On my eighteenth birthday my 'call up' papers came, accompanied by a railway warrant and instructions to report to the 58th Training Regiment (RAC) at Bovington Camp in Dorset. It was Christmas 1941.

In some respects, life in the Army was school all over again, except that my fellow troopers came from all walks of life. I soon learned that it was not always those with the purest of accents who were the most reliable. On our first evening, still dressed in 'civvies', we all went rather shyly to the NAAFI canteen. We sat in a 'rookies' block, overawed by the hairy old sweats around us, some of whom, I found out later, had joined only a few days before us. We exchanged names and I met 'Tiny' Williams, 'Lefty' Thompson, 'Chalky' White, 'Butch' Kemp, 'Sooty' Chapman, 'Halifax' (from that town), Charlie, Winch, Fred, Alf and so on. I was paralysed as my turn approached. My given names were 'Lionel Gale' and I was known by my relations as 'Boy'. I didn't feel that any of these were appropriate to a soldier, but at short notice, my mind couldn't rise above 'Bill', so I announced that as my name and I have retained it happily to this day.

It was one of my father's maxims that if you were asked to volunteer for something then you responded in the affirmative and did your best. I found out very quickly that this was totally opposite to the instructions passed on to their sons by all the other 'dads'. However, it landed me with a lot of jobs, some dull, some interesting. I peeled spuds for the Sergeants' Mess, swept the square for Church Parade, learned some of the intricacies of the camp drains, served drinks in the Officers' Mess (narrowly avoiding becoming a permanent mess waiter) and so on. During this first month I spent my life square-bashing, polishing my equipment and stripping my rifle for inspections. It was not a very exciting time. However, at the end of one of our interminable drill parades the sergeant asked for a volunteer driver. On several occasions I had driven my father's Ford 8 in Wicksteed Park, Kettering, and so I stepped forward. I was then instructed to collect the Scammell recovery truck from the fitters' shop and take it to the Driving and Maintenance Wing in the Main Camp by 0630hrs the following morning. I was numbed by the order, as we had been shown a Scammell and I had the distinct impression that it stood about 10 feet high to the driving platform.

I didn't sleep much that night and at about 0530 hrs I

got up, made up my blankets and in pitch darkness stumbled through the camp to find this monster. I clambered up the steps into the cab and fumbled with the various switches. Eventually a small light came on which I presumed was the ignition. I heaved the great gear lever into what I hoped was neutral and then as I could find no self-starter, I engaged the starting handle at the front under the radiator. I found that it was too stiff for me to turn, so locking it in a horizontal position I stood on it and pushed and jumped with all my force. My guardian angel must have been working overtime, as although the engine turned over with a wheezy slurping noise, it did not fire. If it had done so, I have no doubt that the starting handle would have broken both of my legs. I climbed back into the cabin, pulled out a few more knobs, and then tried the handle again, this time by hand. Suddenly the engine roared into life, throwing me half way across the garage, and the Scammell stood there pulsating and ready to go.

After several false starts we jerked our way out of the garage, turned into the main road through the camp and ground our way through the crowds of recruits on their way to Mess Hall. I felt like a king! As we approached the main gates of our camp, which led out on to the main Bovington–Wool road, I prayed that I wouldn't have to stop. Luckily the regimental policeman opened up the barrier and let me straight through. I crossed the main road in first gear at a majestic 5 miles per hour, and was avoided with great difficulty by a black-bereted officer driving a very elegant Austin 7. He finished up on the grass verge astride a drainage ditch.

At this moment the gates of the D & M Wing opened as if by magic and I juddered through, ground to a halt by the side of the first garage I could find, and ran back towards my own unit. As I reached the gates a very angry officer from the Royal Tank Regiment stopped me. 'Are you the idiot who was driving that Scammell?' he asked. 'Yes, sir' I replied, standing stiffly to attention. 'Why the hell didn't you stop at the main road junction?' the officer continued. It was on the tip of my tongue to tell him, when something stopped me and I remained mute. He then reviewed, in fair detail, my back-ground, breeding, capabilities, likely career as a sanitary orderly, etc! When there was a pause in the ranting, I apologised for my stupidity. He seemed a little taken aback at that and, after one of the amused guards and I had helped him to extract his car and lift it back on to the road, he dismissed me.

At Christmas I had received a postcard from my father indicating that he was in Durban, and it was with surprise that some three weeks later, I had War Office notification that he was posted as missing. However, three months later, in March 1942, I learned that he had been taken prisoner by the Germans and, although wounded, was alive and well. Later I found out that he was captured at Agedabya, where Rommel almost destroyed the 1st Armoured Division. Apparently he and his general swapped cars, and my father then drove across the desert in the staff car flying the command flag. He told me that he felt very important as the German armoured cars turned to chase him; that was, until they opened up with their machine-guns! Happily, the general escaped unscathed.

A few months later, I was learning how to drive a Covenanter tank, taking my turn with the rest of my troop, when the same officer from the Royal Tank Regiment appeared and watched for a short time. He then came over and, calling me out of the ranks, told my sergeant that I was to report to the Main Camp as a relief driver on the tank reliability trial that was being mounted that week. I was, for five days, second driver on a Valentine tank, which, in common with all the other known types, Churchills (with a 2-pounder gun), Covenanters, Crusaders, Honeys,

Shermans, Grants etc., were to be driven, night and day, round a mixed road and cross country course. It was a reliability trial. We completed approximately 1,000 miles together. I contracted diesel oil poisoning and erupted in sores which, as was the custom of the army medical units in those days, were treated with gentian violet. The sores rubbed on the rough material of my battledress and greatcoat. I looked and felt a great mass of violet coloured sepsis and just wanted to hide. However, it was the time of our Passing Out Parade, we had now qualified as soldiers, and we were sent on five days leave. My mother was horrified; I was not attractive to go out with, and although the sores were improving rapidly, I was not unhappy to leave London and return to camp. On my return I found that I had been promoted to Provisional Unpaid Lance Corporal and selected as a potential officer. Later I passed my Commissions Board, and was posted to Sandhurst as an Officer Cadet. It was August 1942.

On arrival at Sandhurst, I was posted to 24 Troop, quickly known as 'The Lords Troop' because it contained so many cadets with titles. I was in 'C' Section, commanded by Captain Julian Ward of the Household Cavalry. Training, under the eagle eye of our sergeant major, Mr Leckie of the Irish Guards, was hard, discipline on the square positively cruel and the level of 'bullshit' required, in terms of both personal kit and the rooms which we occupied, little short of ridiculous. However, we cooperated with enthusiasm and worked very hard at everything they gave us to do. Unfortunately, our exposure to armoured vehicles, gunnery, wireless and driving was minimal. Our exercises were carried out in trucks or on foot, and looking back on it all, we learned very little of technical or tactical value. Most of our troop, having come straight from school or university, had no previous experience to fall back on and I found that on technical matters, having been to a training regiment first, I knew more than most of my colleagues. Despite my boredom and frustration with the drill, the polishing and the scrubbing, I put my heart into it all and undoubtedly left Sandhurst with a more informed and adult approach to problems and their solution.

One of my greatest friends at this time was a fellow cadet, George Atkinson-Willes, whose stepfather, Brigadier John Van der Byl DSO, had commanded the 8th King's Royal Irish Hussars after the First World War. He vetted likely officer recruits for that regiment. George asked which regiment I wished to join and I explained that I wanted to join one which was out in the Middle East and fighting. He invited me to meet the brigadier and I visited him at his large Victorian house in Camberley. He was a kindly old gentleman and, having accepted a fellow cadet, Philip de May, and me as potential officers in the 8th Hussars, invited us to take tea with him at his house every week. He taught us a great deal about the regiment, its traditions and its glorious history. He instilled into me a sense of being a part of this, and I still retain that sense to this day, even though I was finally invalided out of the regiment in 1955. I learnt a lot while I was at Sandhurst, but perhaps the most important lesson of all was that to fail in duty was a dishonour to yourself, your comrades, your regiment and your country. In fact, if the chips were down, then the lives of your soldiers were more valuable than your own. It follows that what some may consider as bravery is in fact the enact-ment of this philosophy of duty.

I worked hard and strove to gain the Sword of Honour for my regiment. In the event and quite rightly it went to 'Poppa' Gowan, an elder statesman of

Regimental badge.

7

perhaps thirty years old, who had a good effect on us all and was a stabilising influence throughout the course. My mother was invited to the Passing Out Parade. She arrived in a stunning hat and dress that defied the war. Despite the cold March day, her ever-present illness – she suffered from *myasthenia gravis* – and her worry that her only child was now likely to have to join the fighting, she brought joy to the event.

After the Passing Out Parade, we all celebrated with 'tea and a wad' in the Old Building. During this party, Captain Ward came over and asked if that pretty woman really was my mother. He then told her that I had been a runner-up for the Sword of Honour. We both believed him, and I know that she felt very proud of me. Looking back on it, perhaps he said that to all the pretty mothers!

It was 15 March 1943 and I left with her to start my first leave as an officer, dressed in the finery of a cornet in the 8th King's Royal Irish Hussars. We spent the week together. My first Paddy's Day (17 March) in the regiment, was spent in Chiswick, with a special lunch of liver, off ration, given to her by colleagues at Smithfield market.

At the end of my leave I reported to the 9th Battalion of the Royal West Kents in Pontefract, as an Assistant Armoured Training Officer. During the train journey north I was sitting opposite an elderly lady, who after some hesitation asked me whether I, as a Polish officer, was enjoying my new life in England. I assured her that I was. It was not the last time that the green and gold tent hat worn by officers in the regiment has been a source of amusement in this way.

I was made very welcome by the Royal West Kents. We did little training, as there was no actual equipment on site, but we had a week at Kirkcudbright Ranges learning some tank gunnery, and did a lot of lorry maintenance. Sleeping, as the officers did, in the jockeys' training room in the grandstand of Pontefract racecourse, I couldn't fail to learn a lot about racing. Happily, meetings were still held there during the war and we had to evacuate our room while the racing was on. I was given some very good tips, as well as

8th KRI Hussar officer's tent hat.

some very bad ones, but all in all it was good fun. We certainly learned to realise how unimportant we all were when the question of our comfort conflicted with the demands of the racing fraternity.

In June, I was posted to the Manchester Regiment in Otley pending overseas posting. This came promptly and I was ordered to liaise with my fellow cadet from Sandhurst, Philip de May, and together we were to proceed to North Africa to join the regiment. We were both granted a week's leave and I visited my old school on the way south.

Arriving unexpectedly at my aunt's house in Kettering, I found my father there. He had been wounded on capture and had been exchanged in Turkey for a boatload of 'mad Italians' (his phrase). After a few weeks convalescence in Cairo, he had been flown home, and his new temporary job was to travel the country giving pep talks to factory workers. He was not very pleased. I enjoyed his account of meeting Rommel, who treated him with great chivalry after his capture, and of the pride with which the Germans presented Major de Patourel with his VC at a parade in Camp 35, Naples, where they were both incarcerated. We spent the remainder of my embarkation leave together in London.

Philip and I met at the RTO's Office in King's Cross station. His air of confidence and calm was very reassuring, and off we went by train. We called them 'Dover' pills as they looked and tasted like chunks of chalk.

At Philippeville, we were directed to a transit camp in a wadi. It was mountainous country, and very hot and arid. I insisted on pitching my tent well up the hillside so as to catch any breeze that existed, while Philip settled down in the valley itself, closer to the Officers' Mess. During the night there was a terrible storm, Philip lost his kit and two soldiers were drowned in their sleeping bags as a torrent of water poured down the old river bed. I tried to join the Green Berets there and be trained for Yugoslavia but the regiment, when contacted, signalled 'No' and they helped both of us to get another train, this time a local to Constantine.

The railway tunnel that leads to that city follows a circular route through the mountains. Our train was full of Arabs, men and women, with chickens, sheep and fleas in abundance. We were scratching within minutes of setting forth. The train had open carriages with a very old steam engine at the front and, when we entered the tunnel, we, literally, nearly choked to death. We both lay on the floor coughing and gasping as we fought for air. Our Arab companions suffered as much as we did and the cries of the people around us added to the general horror. I think this part of the journey lasted for about 30–45 minutes. On emerging, as soon as we could see again, we were astonished at the wonderful view of Constantine, which crowns a mountain top and is surrounded by deep gorges. These were bridged by two very narrow viaducts, one of which carried the railway. It was an unforgettable sight. We reported to the RTO there and then, having obtained a jerrycan of petrol, went into an unoccupied compartment in a siding, stripped, and washed our clothes and ourselves in petrol. We dried them off in the sun and that killed the majority of the bugs.

In the evening we joined a prisoner of war train routed to Tunis, picking up more prisoners at Medjes-el-Bab on the way. Tunis itself was relatively unscathed by the war. I went to the cathedral for mass and met a charming French priest there who gave me a book on Charles de Foucauld, which I still possess. He introduced us to an American Army major who organised a truck to take us from Tunis, via Sousse, to Sfax, where we were stuck and couldn't get any further. It was the end of the line in every way. Luckily I made friends with a naval officer and we sailed a felucca together in the harbour. It was a fascinating boat to sail, as you had to gybe to come about. A little different to our 16-foot lobster boat on the Crouch in Essex. There was, I remember, an Italian hospital ship sunk and on its side just under the water in the harbour. One could see right into the cabins. My naval friend introduced us to his number one and, when their destroyer received orders to sail to Tripoli, they took Philip and me with them.

On arrival in Tripoli, we had the good fortune to fall in with some pilots, who flew Dakotas from the El Adem airport thirty miles south-west of Tripoli. After a couple of very hairy parties with them in the city itself, they uplifted us from our quarters and took us out to their mess. I shared a tent on the airfield with an Australian pilot, who smoked half a Woodbine before going to sleep and placed it over the top of a half a bottle of beer. When he awoke in the morning his hand blindly fumbled for the beer bottle and then, having drunk the tepid flat beer, he smoked the butt end of his cigarette. I couldn't wait to leave. We had two false starts in a Dakota from El Adem, the port engine died on the first and the starboard on the second, and both times we returned to base. On the third all went well until we started to leave the coast for Benghazi, when both engines cut out and we glided to a crash landing on the mud flats near Gabes. Curiously enough, my father had been captured at 'Marble Arch' which

was nearby. Nobody was hurt, so we returned to El Adem by truck, spending a night at the leave centre in Homs on the way. Next day, with some apprehension, we took off again and this time we made it to Benghazi.

As we left the aircraft we were met by the toughest, most bronzed trooper that I had ever encountered. He was wearing the MM. He got out of his jeep, looked us both up and down two or three times, then said 'Cor, f——g schoolboys now', indicated that we should put our kit in the back, and then remained silent until we reached the regimental orderly room. I was mortified. But even more so when it became clear that the adjutant, Jack Ladenburg, was too busy to bother with us. He told us that the regiment had been ordered back to Egypt, and that we were to make our own way there. On arrival in Cairo we were to report to Kasra-Nil Barracks and to find an 8th Hussar officer called Bob Ames. Luckily we were instructed to see Titch Kirkham, the quartermaster, as Philip needed some replacement bedding, and he very kindly sent us in his own truck to the town itself. There we hitched a lift with an American lorry convoy which was just about to leave for the Canal area.

We then enjoyed a fantastic journey along the coasts of Libya and Egypt, and saw clear evidence of the bitter battles that we had read about so often. First Barce, and then Derna with its famous pass, winding tortuously down the mountain side. Terrifying in a 3-ton truck, driven with élan by a black American driver called 'Nutty'. By the end of the 600-mile journey, I realised how he had got his name. We saw Gazala and spent the night close to Sidi Rezegh where the regiment had so distinguished itself. Then on to Sollum and Buq Buq, Sidi Barrani and a final night halt, this time near Mersa Matruh. The next day was especially interesting as we went through the northern end of the site of the battle of El Alamein, where the great turning point in the war had really started.

As we turned south-west towards Cairo, the road surface improved and the speed of the convoy increased. Much of this road was raised above the level of the surrounding desert, with a fall of some 10 to 15 feet on either side. I was in a 3-ton Dodge truck, my back rubbed raw by constant sweaty friction with the leather seat, and my dysentery was becoming menacing again. Suddenly there was an explosion at the front of the vehicle and we slewed off to the right almost turning over in the process. Our front offside tyre had blown. By a stroke of fate, this blew at the very moment that we reached the only place on our side of the road where trucks could park and where the NAAFI had sited a canteen. Apart from damaging the side of another truck, which we hit as we skidded into the car park, we were only shaken and suffered no injury.

On arrival at Kasra-Nil Barracks in Cairo we reported to Bob. I was sent to the MO for a check up, was given a severe rocket for leaving the hospital in Algiers, and finished up in the 15th Scottish Hospital in Alexandria. When I returned, the regiment was installed in a tented camp at Mena, very close to the Pyramids, and I was posted to A Squadron under Major 'Piff' Threlfall. It was October, and rumours began to circulate that we were to return to England and not go to Italy to rejoin the war. I was shattered by this as I felt certain that it would be all over before I had seen any action. I asked if I could be posted to one of the regiments serving in Italy and received an imperial rocket from Colonel Cuthie Goulburn, my commanding officer. I can only remember the last phrases, which were to the effect that he hadn't sent for reinforcements in order to wait for three months while they dawdled across Africa, and then found one of them sick on arrival, only to post them to other regiments. The war in Europe, he added, would more than satisfy my war-fever. I kept a low profile from then on until we transhipped to Port Tewfig, were loaded on to a ship by lighters and, with eighty

junior officers stacked six bunks high in a small cabin, commenced the journey home.

The voyage had its excitements. Our ship rammed the right-hand side of the Suez Canal. Having been towed clear, we joined a convoy off Port Suez and sailed to Malta, which we saw in the early hours. Then north to Famagusta in Sicily, more ships joined us there and we off-loaded some equipment. There were some excitements from aircraft on the voyage to Gibraltar, but after a day standing off that port the convoy reassembled and swung north towards England. It was early December and by this time the seas were fairly heavy. One of the merchantmen, which was returning to England for repairs, suddenly swung to starboard out of the line and rammed another ship. This split the escort and later that night, depth charges exploded alongside our ship as a German submarine attempted to run through the convoy. By this time, I had recurrent dysentery again and collapsed. I ended up in the ship's hospital where they found that I had also contracted a severe case of jaundice. Clearly the heat did not suit my metabolism.

When we arrived in Liverpool I was still too ill to walk and went ashore on a stretcher. Apparently my friends stuffed a load of dutiable goods under the blankets, recovering them as we left customs. The stretcher bearers complained about my weight so there must have been a lot of it! I was taken to Broadgreen Hospital in Liverpool where I stayed until being discharged on 14 January 1944. The staff of that hospital were kindness itself and despite the fact that no one from my family was able to visit me, they made my stay there, including Christmas, a time which I recall with great pleasure.

I left the hospital on a Friday, and travelled down by train to my grandmother's house in Chiswick, with the intention of taking a week's convalescence leave. However, Philip de May telephoned and he told me that there were now a large

number of new officers in the regiment and that the troop leaders appointments were being made. I decided to waive my entitlement to leave and I reported to the adjutant in West Tofts Camp near Thetford, Norfolk, on the Sunday evening. My health was still suspect and in the event I was too late to be given a troop of tanks and instead, to my profound disappointment, was put in charge of A Squadron Echelon.

My mentors were SQMS Jessikins, regimental light heavyweight champion, and Sgt Bob Butterfield. I don't know what they must have thought when they first saw me, but I was very impressed by their experience and I certainly learned a great deal about practical man-management from them both. To my horror, I found that the 15-cwt truck allocated to me at that time was driven by the same trooper who had greeted me when we arrived in Benghazi, Tpr Bob Weir MM. He saluted me most respectfully and then said, 'A little f——r like you needs protection, I'll look after you.' And to be fair, he did that, until he had an altercation with a military policeman just before the invasion and was thrown out of the regiment. Having served his sentence, he came out to the Tank Reinforcement Unit (RFU), but the regiment refused to have him back, and later he collected a DCM for extraordinary bravery while serving with 5th Dragoon Guards.

We trained hard at West Tofts, but only once was I given the chance to command a troop of tanks. This was during an exercise in which we used live ammunition. Under machine-gun fire my driver, with his front visor closed, lost sight of the track, and took us over the edge of a quarry. At the last minute he saw the void in front of us and slewed the tank to the right, one track slipping over the edge, where we teetered for what seemed like a lifetime. I ordered the crew to remain inside and stay totally still, as any movement caused the tank to slip a little more. I then eased myself out of the turret and fixed a tow rope on to the lifting shackle eye on the side of the tank turret and passed it round a tree. This secured it

reasonably safely. I then evacuated the crew and the tank was soon recovered by the LAD. 'I can see why you've got the Transport Troop,' said Bill Best, the LAD Commander.

In late March, we collected the new Cromwell tanks from Leeds and in a regimental convoy returned to West Tofts by road. In April, His Majesty the King visited us, arriving with his escort on the wrong side of the tank park. I was staggered to find him standing next to me as I clambered out from under my truck. 'Where's your commanding officer?' said General Erskine, who was our divisional commander and was escorting the King. 'Please go and fetch him.' The tank park formed a 'U' shape, so I took the direct route across the centre of the 'U' through low bushes and finding the colonel told him of the King's arrival. He too took the quickest route back, and we both arrived with the front of our battledress covered in white fluffy seeds. His Majesty really enjoyed that. Later we were visited by a Russian delegation, who stayed for lunch. The Russian general sat next to the colonel, who at one point, stuck for conversation, pointed to the 'Balaclava' battle honour embroidered on the table cloth in front of him and said, 'We celebrate that as a great victory, general.' 'So do ve, colonel,' replied the general, 'So do ve.'

In April we attended a pep talk, given to all the officers of 7th Armoured Division, by General Montgomery, and shortly afterwards loaded the tanks on to trains at Brandon sidings, where I was thrilled at being allowed to drive a shunting engine for a few miles. The regiment then went by rail to Bognor Regis while the soft vehicles, such as mine, travelled down in convoy by road. We settled down there and completed our programme of waterproofing the vehicles ready for the invasion. Everyone seemed to have a girlfriend and I was lucky to find a kind and gentle girl, Audrey, who seemed to understand my adolescence. Her family were very decent to me as well. I became deeply attached to her, and she became my anchor point in England throughout the ensuing campaign.

Having been put in charge of the squadron echelon I was determined that it would be the best one in the regiment. I studied the problem of refuelling and of the transference of stores to the tanks, and as a result I broke bulk and evolved a new method of stowing ammunition and petrol in my 3-ton lorries. After trials, we proved that this halved the time taken to refurbish a tank, and this was to stand us in good stead later. Initially my squadron leader was furious with me, as it was strictly forbidden to break bulk stores. However, it was too late to alter and he showed off the idea to the colonel, who was cautiously enthusiastic. On 5 June, we were told that the invasion was on. The move to our assembly point was carried out on tracks and wheels during a lovely hot summer's day. There was no parade or crowds to wave us off as we drove through the outskirts of Bognor on to the main road to Chichester and Portsmouth. At one point, as the tanks turned, so the asphalt road surface – which was sticky because of the heat – lifted in great slabs and was distributed generously over the ensuing quarter of a mile. It is an indication of the pragmatic attitude of the residents that a bill for this damage reached the regiment during the battles in the Bocage!

We spent that night in the New Forest and from there to Gosport where we drove to 'Bumper' quay and embarked for France. I have a note of the orders given at that time and they read:

TT's 111 and 114 alongside 50509 on BUMPER
Move off 1110hrs tomorrow (A RCRP4 1140hrs)
Parade 0945hrs Regtl Parade Ground (D Sec)
All men have Embarkation Tags with them.
1400hrs Map Distribution and Briefing.
1630–1800hrs Stores by Crafts.
Bellamy   Fry

Jessikins   Wizard
Butterfield   Cook
Rations 43 men – 5 Boxes –
Split 'B' Echelon – 1, 'A1' Echelon – 2, 'A2' Echelon – 2

I was twenty years old. I tried to conceal my excitement with a veneer of sophistication, but in reality I couldn't wait for it all to begin. To me, it seemed like a sort of game, there was a feeling of chivalry about it, almost a crusade and certainly a sense of heroism at being part of it. It didn't reduce my awareness of the dangers, nor did it make me careless, but I decided that if I had to take risks in order to carry out my allocated task, then right was on our side, and they would be well worth taking.

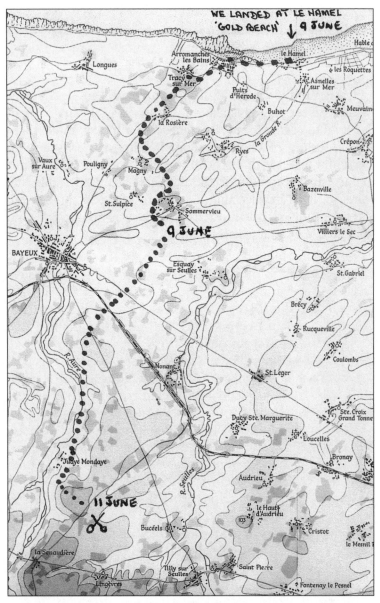

Battle for Villers Bocage

TWO

Transport Troop, A Squadron

Only a very dull-witted or totally unimaginative person would have remained calm and unexcited by the prospect of taking part in the invasion. The atmosphere was electrifying, not only because of the long wait and the huge build-up, but also by the very nature of the task facing us all. It was a great leap into the unknown, and my imagination ran wild at the thought of all the incredible and exciting things that I might find when we landed. This excitement did not diminish after we had embarked, in fact rather to the contrary, it gained in intensity as we began to see evidence of the enormous fleet of ships which was engaged in this operation.

It was exhilarating, it was a challenge, and it was the objective for which we had been training during the past months and years. For the first time it was not an 'exercise' but it was real, and the bullets and the various weapons which we would use would call for a response in kind from the enemy. Many soldiers in the regiment knew from experience what that was like and how they would react to it. I was not one of them. I was fortunate in that my youth and inexperience did not permit me to think too deeply about the possible hazards. I was excited, keen to prove myself, and still somewhat disappointed that my command was unlikely to involve me in any front line fighting. Commanding the squadron echelon, although vitally important, did not have the same cachet as that of commanding a troop of tanks. This was not a view shared by 'Titch' Kirkham, the diminutive but competent and experienced captain who commanded the regimental echelon. He assured me that I would soon see enough action to satisfy my needs and 'One day, I would be bloody glad that I stayed with his command.' I must have been a very irritating young man to have around at this time, as he had plenty to occupy him without the added burden of my desire to win the war on my own.

Although the 'O' Group had settled all the details of loading personnel and vehicles, allocation of rations, etc., it did not tell us what we were to do when we had arrived on the beach. We knew what sort of country to expect, but a map reference of the site for our eventual leaguer could not be given until we had actually arrived. The notes which I took at that briefing proved to be surprisingly accurate. They read: 'Country – small fields, narrow, banked, thick-bushy, well-treed roads. Many orchards but few woods, only scrub land. Hundreds of houses, hamlets and small villages. Small rivers running from south to north these are shallow with boggy surrounds.' They go on to note that 7th Armoured Division, of which we were the armoured reconnaissance regiment, were to fight to 'capture Villers-Bocage and Mount Pinçon'. We would 'Concentrate north of Bayeux probably'. Somewhat later I received instructions to rendezvous with Titch as soon as the vehicles had left the beach and that 'we would play it from there'. The remainder of the notes concerned the arrangements for embarking on the tank landing craft.

My troop was to be split over two craft, TT 111 and TT 114, these would be alongside 'Bumper' quay in Gosport harbour and we were to embark, starting at 1101hrs on 8 June. We were at this time assembled in a marshalling area in the New Forest. There was some delay, but we left

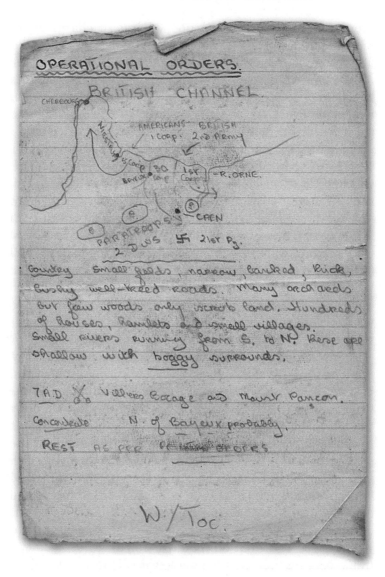

Original notes taken at 'O' Group on 6 June 1944.

eventually in the early afternoon. I was in charge of 43 men and 15 soft vehicles. These included the squadron fitters as well as lorries which belonged to A and B Echelons. A Echelon, which was my troop, comprised those vehicles which were to service the squadron in the field. B Echelon was made up of the vehicles involved in the back-up, and they were ultimately under the command of Titch. I allocated SQMS Jessikins to TT 111 and Sgt Davies to TT 114. Every man was issued with an embarkation tag, which was handed to the embarkation officer as we went on board, thus recording each individual's actual departure. Finally, just before loading men and vehicles, we were issued with five boxes of rations to see us through the next two days. Once aboard, we were kept very busy securing vehicles and checking that everything was in order, and I was surprised when I found that we had left Gosport and were already well out into the harbour. I saw the shape of the gun-towers as we went out into the Solent, joining a long line of similar vessels. Then darkness fell and we could see no more.

To my astonishment and to the eternal credit of the Navy, the journey to France was devoid of any major excitements. We saw debris and at one point some bodies floating in the water, but there was no attack either by enemy aircraft or by their torpedo boats. Our Royal Navy commander was as hospitable as any man could have been under the circumstances. We were offered drinks and warmth in the tiny cabin. He was obviously sorry for us and voiced his happiness at returning back to England as soon as he had deposited us on the beach. I suppose that I did sleep a little during the crossing, but as soon as the first glimmer of light was detected I was out on the deck watching the volume of traffic pouring over the Channel towards France. This whole area of sea became more and more like Piccadilly Circus as we ploughed on in lines, with ships of all shapes and sizes bustling about around us. It was all very impressive.

In the meantime the sound of the naval guns, which had grown louder by the minute, confirmed the presence of several cruisers and destroyers, all firing in the direction of France. It was getting lighter by this time, and I noticed that the water was changing to a more muddy colour so I knew that we had nearly arrived. The sense of expectancy began to bubble over inside me and it was almost a relief when suddenly someone pointed excitedly and shouted, 'There's the coast,' and there it was, the coastline of France ahead of us. It looked featureless and more like the arrival at Ostend than the sort of skyline that I had envisaged. Our LCT drew into line with several others, which were being marshalled by a very busy corvette, itself off-loading infantry into smaller landing craft. The sea seemed to be full of wrecks and flotsam, with stranded ships apparently stuck in the sand all around us. Our captain was having difficulty in finding a way through all these hazards, but I was more thrilled by the sound of the guns onshore. This really was war.

I was not certain whether 8th Hussar officers wore tin hats or not. This is one of my main recollections of the last few minutes prior to landing. I wanted to do the right thing. I decided to land wearing my green and gold side hat and stuffed my tin hat under the seat of my jeep. Then the captain gave me the prearranged warning signal and I ordered everyone to mount their vehicles, warm-up their engines and then switch off. Shortly after this, the rear anchor of TT 111 was dropped, this was to enable them to kedge the ship off the beach after the disembarkation had been completed. By now we were 100 yards from the shore and I gave the order to start the engines again. My jeep was the first in line for disembarkation and as the front of the LCT banged down we drove straight out into about three feet of water.

The bottom was firm and my driver, Cpl Fry, was very experienced. There was no hesitation and we shot out of the wet in a cloud of spray on to softish dry sand. The beach itself shelved gently up to a sea wall and as we got closer to that, urged on by the beach marshals, I saw that there were steel mesh frames laid on top of the sand hills to give added traction. I started to pull over to the left before reaching these, in order to check that all my vehicles had landed, but an angry marshal waved me on. I told Fry to slow down and I shouted back that I must collect my troop together. 'Not on MY beach, sonny,' came the reply as he thumped the side of the vehicle, and we drove on. As we got into the dunes I noticed the first evidence of battle, with burnt-out vehicles and general debris mixed into the German barbed wire entanglements. These bore the sign 'Achtung Minen!!' I hoped that there were none left on the road.

Our jeep bounced its way up the ramp and after about 200 yards we debouched on to a track running away to the right, in what I presumed was the general direction of Bayeux. We had landed near a tiny village called Le Hamel, but were not allowed any time to investigate as the pressure of the traffic forced us forward. The road was very narrow and climbed away sharply up a hillside for about 400 yards, before cresting the hill and swinging away to the left behind the larger fishing village of Arromanches. I remember a church just to the left of this road which seemed to be relatively undamaged. There were signs everywhere, beach signs, warnings of mines, signs indicating various services; there were great dumps of ammunition and petrol, stores dumps, a field hospital; and mixed up with all this were sappers and infantry, tanks and artillery, trucks and a host of 'Ducks' (amphibious vehicles which seemed to occupy the whole road). It was very bewildering. I was unable to stop because of the pressure of vehicles behind me, and yet I was anxious to ensure that my troop was all safely ashore. Eventually, I managed to pull into the entrance of a stores dump and to my relief all eight of my trucks eventually appeared. I told the leading truck to continue along the road for a mile and then pull into the side and collect the others. I would then catch them up and tell them what we were to do.

I waited for a few minutes by the roadside, but there was no sign of Titch or indeed any members of our party so I felt somewhat at a loss. However, to my joy, just before I caught up with the rest of the troop, I saw a 7th Armoured Divisional sign, the Desert Rat. This indicated that I was on the divisional centre line (each division marked the central road or track running through its planned line of advance) and thus, if I followed those, I would be sure to find the regiment. The troop fell in behind me and joined the column of vehicles going inland. After a few miles we saw an 8th Hussar tank whose crew told us that the main body was harbouring in a orchard near a village called 'Something View'. I couldn't find this on the map at first but then noticed Sommervieu, just off the Bayeux road.

We found the regiment pulled into a large field and tucked into the hedges. Everyone was hard at work removing the waterproofing from their tanks. There were thousands of other troops about and great competition to find somewhere to stop. I tried to pull into the field with my vehicles, but was told by one of the regimental police that the echelon was elsewhere and I was to go back and find it. At that moment the colonel appeared accompanied by the adjutant, Jack Ladenburg, who beckoned to me to come over. I leapt down from my jeep and was astonished to be instructed to find divisional headquarters and report personally to General Erskine that the regiment had arrived. When I asked Jack where they were, he told me to follow the divisional centre line. Later I discovered that there was wireless silence, that I had not been especially selected for the honour but was the first officer to arrive with a non-armoured vehicle who had nothing to do. The story of my life!

'...in a cloud of spray on to softish dry sand.'

I set off with Fry, feeling very full of the importance of my mission and we made good progress through the traffic, which soon began to thin out. There was a lot of noise from our guns, and artillery units seemed to be in every field. We had a moment of thrill when a German fighter aircraft shot overhead, very low, coming from the direction of the beachhead but heading towards his own lines. There was no sign of divisional HQ but I saw another Desert Rat sign so I knew that we were on the correct road. The next sign appeared to point off the Bayeux road to the right, so we turned off and, as there was no traffic, started to speed up.

After a couple of miles I began to get a little apprehensive as I had seen nothing but the occasional vehicle and no field guns or infantry. Happily, we came upon a squadron of 5th Royal Tank Regiment; a major with a mapboard in hand stood by one of the tanks, so we stopped and he asked us where we were going. I told him that I was looking for divisional HQ and had just landed. He advised me to return the way that I had come and fast. He added that I was now on the outskirts of Sully, which was still occupied by the

Germans, and his squadron formed part of an attack which was due to go in at any minute. We swung round and drove back to the T-junction and, ignoring the offending sign, turned towards Bayeux once more. We found divisional HQ a short distance down the road on the left-hand side with the two ACVs parked in a field.

I jumped out of the jeep, reporting to the RMP that I had a message for the general and ran towards the command vehicles. They looked enormous to me and I was heavy with apprehension as to my message and how to present it. I felt rather important and romantic, a slight 'Hero of Peninsular War galloped in with vital message' feeling overcame me. As I hesitated outside the first of the ACVs, the general happened to come down the steps, accompanied by his G.1 (divisional chief of staff) and seeing me asked, most courteously, what I wanted. 'I have the honour to report, sir, that 8th Hussars have landed and are in the harbour at Sommervieu,' I said, standing stiffly to attention after giving him my best and most punctilious salute. 'Good God, man,' said the general, 'I don't want any more bloody tanks, give me 131 Brigade.' (131 Brigade was the divisional infantry brigade, most of which had not yet landed.) I was somewhat nonplussed by his reaction and obviously looked a bit dejected, because he then smiled, thanked me for my report and asked me to convey his good wishes to Colonel Cuthie. It was all over in a matter of seconds but I certainly sensed that he was a worried man and in a peculiar way that made me even more determined to pull my weight. I saluted and turned to go, but the G.1 told me to go to ACV2 and see the G.2 who would give me some papers for personal delivery to the colonel. I collected these and then went back to Sommervieu, where I found that the de-waterproofing of the tanks was approaching completion. I reported the general's words to Jack and handed over the envelope. He in turn told me where I would find my troop and indeed the whole of the regimental echelon, and off I went to spend my first night in France. I was very tired indeed, and even the excitement of being in a battlefield didn't keep me awake.

The next two days, 9 and 10 June, were occupied in routine tasks, de-waterproofing the vehicles and checking that everything was properly stowed. Both A and B Echelons stayed near to the beachhead, the source of supplies, while the regiment moved several times, eventually finishing up just south of Bayeux. I visited the squadron each day. On the second day they were in a large gently sloping hay field, which had just been cut. Regimental HQ was hidden in the hedgerows of this field sharing them with 'A' Squadron, whose HQ was on the far side. Camouflage was not very strict at this time, as we were about three miles behind the lines, to the north of Tilly-sur-Seulles, and we rarely saw enemy aircraft. I left my jeep and the driver by the entrance, and walked across the field towards the squadron. I had gone about half way when there was the most tremendous screaming roar and a huge spray of earth spewed up under the point where my right foot was just about to descend. I stood there, on one leg, rooted to the spot, then I realised that it was a spent shot that had missed me, I was still alive and could go on again. All around the field there were roars of laughter and when, with a rather red face, I eventually reached the squadron, I was told that I had stood there riveted to the spot for about twenty minutes. Probably a slight exaggeration! Apparently, 8th Armoured Brigade were involved in a bitter battle for Tilly-sur-Seulles, which was taking place a few miles to the south of us and we were getting the 'overs' from the German 88mm guns. After I returned to the echelon, I heard that they became so bad that the regiment was forced to move to another leaguer.

During 11 and 12 June the regiment acted as right flank guard to the division, while other regiments were involved in an attack in the general direction of Tilly-sur-Seulles and

Villers-Bocage. I drove out in my jeep each day and got to know the narrow twisting roads quite well. I learned some very useful local geography, which was to stand me in good stead later; practised a bit of schoolboy French on the few civilians I met; and became at ease in the climate of 'behind the lines'. I also became conversant with names which I would never forget, such as Abbaye Mondaye with its huge domed abbey and long stone wall, Trungy, St Paul de Vernay and so on. During my visit to the squadron on 12 June, my squadron leader, Piff Threlfall, told me that the regiment would be taking part in a major attack the next day and that the squadron would need to be refuelled on the 13th. I would get my orders from Titch Kirkham, as the supply would be organised at a regimental level.

I returned to the echelon and was told that 'A' Squadron was to lead the attack and would need to be refuelled separately as their centre line would probably change. Titch told me to go with the other squadron echelon to a point near Abbaye Mondaye, later a focal point for tank routes, and wait for instructions. I had a wireless set in the jeep. At about midday the advance started. I had already tuned into the forward wireless net and listened to the reports of the battle. I was unable to hear the squadron itself, but from the one-sided conversations that I did hear, I gathered that there had been casualties. Wireless contacts became so bad that I decided to move forward. I selected one of the minor roads running south on which I had travelled earlier. By these means I regained contact and was able once again to hear some of the talk on the forward link. However I was out of touch with Titch because of the distance, although at one point in the afternoon I heard him call for all echelons to return. I kept this news to myself, as I decided that it didn't apply to us. The regiment would certainly need to be refuelled and as we were the only echelon in the area I stayed where I was. The range of our 19 sets was very short especially in such close country, all wireless messages were difficult to read and I had every excuse.

At about 1500hrs I decided that I should move my chaps closer to the front and I joined the minor road running from Villers-Bocage to Bayeux near the village of Trungy. It was a particularly bad, narrow, twisting minor road, bounded by high-hedged banks. There was absolutely no traffic but the ground was very low-lying, following a small stream along a valley, and I lost all wireless contact. I continued to drive down one of the tracks, following traces of tanks, crossed the main road from Tilly to St-Lô and eventually arrived at some higher ground near La Butte crossroads. Here, we broke out into a patch of relatively open country, and at the top of a small rise, I stopped and tried once more to contact Titch on the wireless, but there was no response. However, on switching back to the forward link, I heard what I took to be preliminary instructions for the regiment to leaguer for the night in the area of Livry crossroads. I decided to stay where I was and await developments, as Livry crossroads were only about three miles away. All the time there was firing both to our front and to our left, but even at the short distance that we were from the actual fighting, one could not really gauge its intensity. I felt totally at ease and in control of my situation. My troop seemed to be happy and relaxed, and we were all enjoying the warm sun and the blue sky.

At about 1900hrs I warned everybody to be ready to move in an hour's time. Being in the echelon had some perks and we ate a good hot meal cooked on what I had learned was the standard form of soldiers' stove. This comprised a jerrycan, cut in half, filled with earth and then topped up with petrol. The jerrycans were not like those that one saw later in the war, they were oblong, disposable and made out of thin gauge metal. To open them, one prised off the lid with a screwdriver. It made a very quick, hot and effective form of cooking stove, but was dangerous to the unwary. Later that month, my tank driver, Chamberlain, was badly burned when, having primed the stove with petrol, he took the half empty jerrycan and laid it down behind him. Unbeknownst to him, a trail of petrol led from the stove to the jerrican, and when he threw a match on to the stove, the jerrycan blew up. His resultant injuries were so severe that he had to be evacuated and didn't return to the crew until September.

At 2000hrs I had a long discussion with Bob Butterfield and studied the map for the umpteenth time. The last news from the regiment put them in an area south of Livry, perhaps up to six miles from our present position. I felt, from what I had heard on the wireless, that they would be disengaging at nightfall and then go into leaguer. The question was, where exactly would they settle? I decided that they would stick to the minor roads adjacent to the centre line, which I had been given at the original 'O' Group. We would be best therefore, to feel our way forward, hoping to see signs of regimental HQ or of one of the squadrons before we had gone too far. By this time the sound of gunfire was sporadic, although there still seemed to be heavy fighting going on both to our left, towards Tilly-sur-Seulles, and away to our right, in the American area.

In the end I decided that it would be wise for the lorries to stay where they were, temporarily, while I went forward in my jeep and tried to locate the regiment before nightfall. Luck was on my side, as at about 2100hrs I saw the tanks of RHQ just off the road near Livry itself. I reported to the adjutant, who told me that the colonel had gone to brigade HQ to get new orders, but that he thought that they were likely to leaguer somewhere in their present area. He said that the tanks were needing both petrol and ammunition, but that the last thing they wanted was a gaggle of soft vehicles to protect at the moment. There were enemy everywhere and the line was very ill defined. I waited for some time but as there was no news as to when exactly the colonel might return, and it was getting dark, I requested permission to return to my troop, move a little closer, and await events. Jack agreed but added that he would give us the map reference of the leaguer as soon as he received it, but that we were not to move until we knew to where we had to go. He also said that, in view of the delays, they wouldn't be in the leaguer until after midnight.

By the time I returned to the troop I was out of wireless contact again, although the distances were not great. I changed position several times but couldn't raise them, we were very bothered by static, morse and general fuzz on our set. I sat tight until midnight, no message was received and, curiously enough, we heard no tank movement. I decided that under the circumstances it was vital to find them at all costs and so, nose to tail, we crawled slowly forward in the darkness. Map reading was difficult, there was only a minute light in the front of my jeep and I daren't have that on for too long. It is very difficult to judge distance at night and there were neither road signs nor indeed signs of any other units in the area. We had become accustomed to seeing lights glimmering under upturned jerrycans with a unit number punched in the side of the tin, which identified the unit that was parked there. I could not allow even sidelights on the trucks as we were so close to the enemy lines. The strain on the drivers was terrific. I became very conscious of the loud grinding noises that Bedford trucks make when they are in low gear, and felt that the Germans must know exactly where we were and what we were doing.

By about 0130hrs we had fumbled and ground our way through the tiny lanes, without seeing a soul, and had reached the crossroads before the village of Livry. There we were challenged by a very nervous platoon of infantry, who were on guard. I told them that we were 8th Hussar Echelon and asked the platoon sergeant whether he had seen any guide from the regiment or if he knew where the regiment was. He told me that his instructions were that all the echelons had been recalled as division was keeping the roads clear for troop movement. I said that, as we were so close to the regiment, it would be safer and more sensible for us to go to them than to try to drive back in the dark. He took the point and suggested that we turned left towards Juvigny and Tilly. He thought that there were tanks there somewhere but he did not know exactly how far along they were.

We ground on slowly and I tried to calculate our progress. I had instructed the drivers to follow my jeep closely but, after about twenty minutes with no sign of the regiment or indeed any other unit, I stopped and ran down the column telling everyone to sit tight, to switch off and to keep quiet. I then asked Bob Butterfield, who was in the rear 3-tonner, to join me at the front of the convoy so that we could discuss the situation. Both of us felt that we had travelled between two and three miles and were approaching the crossroads at La Butte. We were all well aware that the battle had been fought around Granville, while Hottot, perhaps three miles further on, was marked on my map as in enemy hands. Nothing that I had heard on the wireless had led me to believe that this situation had changed during the day. We had seen no British army unit sign since we had left the crossroads at Livry and we both had a nasty suspicion that we were in no man's land, but equally could be behind the German front line. I felt that the next junction would be in enemy hands, as the last information received from the regiment indicated that both sides were withdrawing to their night positions.

Suddenly we heard the splutter of a motorcycle engine a few hundred yards down the road. My driver had fought in the desert and he exclaimed, 'My God, that's a German bike.' I believed him, as there were not many motorcycles in the British Army, except in the military police, and I thought it was unlikely that one would be in that area at 0230hrs.

Luckily the noise faded into the distance, so whoever it was didn't trouble us. Nevertheless I decided that we should turn round. This proved to be a most complex operation, not only because of the darkness, but also because there was no wide spot in the road where we could manoeuvre. Eventually, I discovered a gateway about 50 yards ahead and having reversed into it, I placed Bob Butterfield in the leading vehicle and the convoy drove past me. I then drove out, returning to help the other vehicles to reverse into the gap, then to turn and re-form behind my jeep. As each truck reached its appointed position it was told to switch off so as to minimise the noise. The plan worked well and everybody made the turn despite the difficulties. When we had re-formed I ran down the line and told each driver to start up and then move off at the same time as the truck in front in tight formation. I got into my jeep, Fry started the engine and we moved slowly forwards. Suddenly, a flare shot up into the air and the night became as day. We were all just on the move at the time and it had a staggering effect on the speed of everyone's departure. As we all accelerated, so there were bursts of rifle or machine gun fire from the fields on both sides but slightly to our rear. Clearly none of the shots came anywhere near us, as no one was hit and no damage was noted to any of the vehicles, but it was very enervating at the time. Curiously enough, it helped us to get away, because for about half a minute we could actually see the vehicle in front. Then, equally suddenly, we were plunged into darkness again. It seemed even more impenetrable after the brightness of the light of the flare.

Once we were round the corner I felt relatively safe, but rather than risk the chance of an enemy patrol catching up with us I decided to continue on slowly back towards Livry crossroads and have another think. We were within several hundred yards of it when a corporal, who turned out to be a guide from the regiment, flagged us down. We had passed them once again. We drove on to the crossroads, turned and went back down the road for the third time. After about 500yds we saw, on the left-hand side, the 45 sign of the 8th Hussars, it was well set back in the hedgerow and almost invisible unless pointed out to you. By now it was about 0300hrs and I was very relieved to have found them. The guide arrived back at the leaguer at the same moment as we did. He had been down the centre-line to look for us, but, presumably, left after we had passed the entrance, and so we had missed each other.

I went over to the RHQ tanks and woke Jack. Apparently he had only been in bed for a few minutes as Orders had not finished until about half an hour previously. He, semi-joking, asked me what the hell I was doing swanning about in soft vehicles in the front line at this time of night. Then Colonel Cuthie appeared. He was obviously delighted that we had found them and asked if I had sufficient on board to refuel and rearm the whole regiment. I replied that we would certainly try and we got at it with a will. The tank crews were dead on their feet but once roused they buckled to as well and we had the whole job finished in under an hour. I was pleased, because the special method that I had developed at Bognor, whereby all the trucks were full of ammunition in racks instead of boxes, and petrol was stacked so that it was ready to load into the tanks, worked like a charm. The sad news from A Squadron was that Bill Talbot-Hervey was dead, as were many of his troop, and Douglas Rampf was seriously wounded. This made a great gap in the friends with whom I had been happily associated in the squadron and suddenly, and for the first time, the war became more bitter and personal.

It was nearly 0400hrs by this time, and my seven trucks were almost empty. As dawn broke, we drove out of the gateway and turned back towards the crossroads and Bayeux. All the drivers were weary, the narrow road twisted and turned, dust blew around us and the sun grew quickly in its intensity. My heart missed a beat when a troop of light tanks appeared round the corner ahead of us. Happily for us they were part of Recce Troop of 5th Royal Tanks and they were kind enough to pull into a nearby field to let us through. We were beginning to feel that home was in sight by this time and were driving along in close convoy at about 20mph. I could almost taste my breakfast and feel the bliss of my bedding roll back at base. As we approached Les Maréchoux, the road narrowed and dipped to the right, followed by a blind left-handed corner at the bottom. I rounded this and nearly went through the windscreen as Fry jammed on the brakes. The oncoming Bren gun carrier, which we only just avoided, stood on its nose and rocked, as only those ungainly but practical vehicles can, while another one rammed it in the rear. At the same time there was a ghastly crunch behind me as three of my trucks, with their drivers half asleep, ran into the back of the one in front. In a matter of seconds we had chaos. Worse however was to come, as standing up in the front of the leading Bren gun carrier was the brigade commander of 131 Brigade. Apparently a battalion of the Queens had just landed and were being rushed up to the front to fill the gap in the divisional centre. He was not pleased with me, and in a few seconds destroyed any composure that I had gained. The essence of his remarks was that the road had been cleared for him, I had no right to be on it and by God I'd get off it now or he'd have my balls for breakfast. I tried to explain what had happened but he hadn't time to listen and ordered me to drive or, 'Bloody well carry my lorries off the road.' When I pointed out to him that this meant putting them all into the ditch as we couldn't reverse, he said so-be-it or words to that effect. The Bren gun carriers rattled and clattered past, and within five or ten minutes the road was clear again and we stood miserably by our wrecked trucks in the silence left by their departure.

I attempted to re-form my little convoy, but two of the 3-tonners and the 15-cwt water truck were inextricably stuck. No recovery vehicles or other forms of help appeared and curiously enough, the road was once again completely silent and deserted. I felt desolate but as usual the soldiers were marvellous and joked their way out of the problems. I left the three trucks without a guard, piled everyone into the other vehicles and we arrived back at base at about 1100hrs absolutely exhausted. We were both surprised and delighted at our welcome. Instead of a rocket for smashing up the trucks and failing to obey the orders given over the wireless, we were acclaimed as the heroes of the hour. Apparently an appreciative message had been received from RHQ and to my astonishment, I didn't even get a ticking off from Titch for leaving the three lorries, but was commended for having stuck at it and located the regiment. Actually this was a very interesting lesson to me in that, in war, equipment is expendable in the interests of survival. Titch sent the fitters out to recover the vehicles and I was told to get my head down. I woke up later that evening and found that all the trucks had been recovered, the squadron echelon had been reloaded with stores and my dinner was ready. It had been a very exciting 24 hours.

Since writing this, Colonel Cuthie Goulburn has given me the following extract from his diary which was written at the time:

12th June – I returned to RHQ from this conference (Brigade H.Q. – Brigadier Hinde) and found them getting into leaguer. By the time I have given out orders for tomorrow it is nearly 2 a.m. I am worried that the replenishment lorries will try to find us in the area where A Squadron pushed up tonight. If so, they may well run into the enemy. Bellamy the Echelon commander, had arrived up at RHQ at 9 p.m. and had been told by Jack Ladenburg that we should be leaguering in that area. We cannot raise Bellamy on the wireless set to tell him of our new leaguer area. So I sent a reliable guide back down to centre line to stand by the side of the road and to intercept the echelon without fail. He is successful at 3 a.m. and at 3.30 a.m. they arrive in our leaguer. Drivers are awakened and they fill up with petrol. I sleep the last hour of the night (3.30–4.30 a.m.) in peace.

The next day was fraught with rumour. The battle of Villers-Bocage was under way and there were stories of regiments being decimated. I was on tenterhooks, not improved by the echelon being ordered to move to an orchard about three miles to the west of Bayeux, which was nowhere near the battle. Titch was adamant that nobody should leave camp. There would be no visits to the regiment and he would allow no variation to this rule until the colonel had given him new instructions. We were all on edge that day, news was scarce, and yet from the casualties that we saw coming back through to the field hospital we knew that fighting was fierce. Eventually we heard that the casualties were less than we had feared, but that the 4th County of London Yeomanry had been caught in Villers-Bocage by two German armoured divisions and were virtually written off. This turned out to be reasonably accurate, although a large number of the members of that regiment managed to escape on foot and returned to our lines.

We spent a restless night, but in the morning RHQ contacted Titch, asking him to send an officer up as soon as possible so that he could be given new instructions. It was agreed that I should go, as I was conversant with the roads in the area where RHQ was expected to be. I decided to take LCpl Holden with me, as he was a wireless operator and a very good map-reader. We jumped into our jeep at about 1000hrs, checked the wireless and drove off down the road in the direction of Villers-Bocage. It was, I remember, another really brilliant sunny day, and the trees and hedgerows were covered in thick dust generated by all the heavy traffic which was travelling down every designated major road within the bridgehead. It was a real relief to turn off the main highway and follow the winding narrow road which led southwards. Those villages, which had seemed so new and so strange two days before, appeared as old friends welcoming us on our journey.

There was little traffic as we passed over La Butte crossroads, and I noticed that the divisional HQ was now sited there, which gave me some confidence that we were on a cleared road this time. Then, on to the crossroads at Livry, where Bill Talbot-Hervey had been killed and Douglas Rampf knocked out and wounded earlier in the week. The guns were very active around us and, although we were unable to see anything of the battle, it was obvious that the artillery were being offered plenty of targets. We could hear the sharper crack of tank guns but they were further away and to the south-east. Our progress was being slowed up by this time as there were other vehicles churning about in the area. Because of this, it was not until 1400hrs that we discovered the sign and the track which led down to RHQ. They were situated together with B Squadron, in the inevitable orchard.

There was plenty of activity and, as we arrived, some very accurate shelling began and we all took such cover as we could find. I tried to report to the colonel but everybody was busy, so I sat by his tank waiting and listened on one of the RHQ wireless sets to the battle going on just to the south of us. A Squadron was in the thick of it, it seemed that the enemy were mounting a fierce counterattack and that they had made some gains.

I was enjoying a mug of tea when the shelling suddenly intensified; it was very close this time, with shells falling among the tanks and killing or injuring a number of members of the regiment. The squadron leader of B Squadron, Punch Dunne, received a wound in the same leg in which he had been wounded in Egypt. While the shelling was on, I was lying directly behind the tanks and as I got up I found that I was standing next to Colonel Cuthie. He looked at me and said 'Ah . . . John . . . you're here . . . well done . . . jolly good,' and that was it. I was elated, as that was the first time that the colonel had called me by my Christian name and, although it was the wrong name, I felt that it still meant that I was now an accepted member of the team. Then Jack came over to me and told me that the regiment was to retire to a leaguer in the area of La Butte and that they would require a complete replenishment. I was to arrange for a cooked hot meal to be available. My map was marked up and I was about to leave when Colonel Cuthie came over and said that there were a number of German infantry about and I was not to go yet. It appeared that snipers had actually infiltrated our lines, which were adjacent to those of brigade HQ.

I settled down to wait and a few minutes later, heard that Mike Browne, another of my friends and a very capable troop leader in A Squadron, had just been killed. I was devastated, that was three out of the five troop leaders in A Squadron killed or wounded in two days of action. I had hardly assimilated this news when Jack came over and told me that Philip de May, with whom I had shared all the excitements of the journey out to join the regiment in Egypt, had just been killed by the shelling within the leaguer. War does not allow much time for mourning; this, I have found, comes later when one has time to reflect. Jack told me to leave at once, adding that I was to inform Titch Kirkham that I would be leaving the echelon forthwith to become a replacement troop leader as soon as A Squadron had had a chance to reorganise.

We drove out of the orchard, my mind filled with sadness at the death of so many of my friends, most of them experienced troop leaders and, in my judgement anyway, experts in tank warfare. I often found during the war that I was able to stand back and look at the scene around me as if I was not actually a participant but that it was all a dream. This was one of those occasions, when a sense of unreality pervaded and I felt out of touch with self, a sort of 'sugary' feeling came over me as if I was being manipulated gently into doing something which I wanted to do, but over which I had no control. At the same time, my practical self was trying to come to terms with my appointment as a tank troop leader. The idea pleased me very much, but I was very conscious both of my lack of practical experience and the undoubted fact that I would have remained in the echelon if my friends had not been casualties. I was certainly much more apprehensive of my possible failure to make the grade, than of any feeling of personal fear at the dangers inherent in the job itself.

The narrow cart track which I was following ran by the side of a bank topped by a rough hedge, and then debouched on to the minor road, almost a track itself, running between Villers-Bocage and Livry. There was no traffic and there was a lull in the gunfire, the early evening sunshine was blazing down as if nothing had happened and the world was still at peace. We reached the road junction, stopped momentarily and then turned left. I was driving and gradually started to speed up. There were soldiers on the verges on both sides of the road, some in the hedgerow itself and some in a file marching towards Livry. Holden was sitting quietly beside me wearing earphones and I glanced across at him to indicate that I was going to pull out to pass the infantry column when I suddenly realised that the soldiers were wearing green uniforms and I was driving quietly along in the middle of a company of German infantry. At that point I was almost face to face with one of them, who regarded me with the same look of astonishment on his face that I must have worn myself. Instinctively I accelerated, putting my foot down and we shot through the column, narrowly missing the leader. The road opened up marginally and there was a wide grass verge on the left followed by a sharp right-hand bend. In my excitement I over-steered, swerved and hit the grass verge hard so that we bounced up into the air just in front of the soldiers, and then veered across the road into the corner. There was a belated burst of Schmeisser fire which didn't touch us, and then an enormous bang and a cloud of smoke and debris which seemed to be on the nose of the jeep. I felt a terrific crack on the head and we skidded round the corner and out of sight of the enemy. Holden was holding on to the jeep clutch-bar like grim death itself, he'd lost his beret, his earphones had gone and his Sten gun, which had been lying across his lap, clattered out on to the road behind us. A number of other items had been thrown out as we bounced, but the map board was still intact and stuck firmly down the side of my seat next to the gearbox. I felt very dazed, and initially I wondered if I had misread the map and somehow had turned towards Villers-Bocage and the battle, instead of away from it.

By this time I could feel blood running down my face and see it dripping on to my battledress front, so, having rounded another corner and seeing no more enemy, we stopped and Holden took over the driving. We decided to drive on cautiously and had only gone about a quarter of a mile when we met a patrol of the Queens who were taking up a defensive position astride the road ready for the withdrawal. Luckily they identified us as friendly straight away, otherwise we should have been shot up again. They were very kind, saw that I had been wounded and helped me out on to the verge while we told them of the enemy infantry approaching. I sat on the grass feeling rather sorry for myself, as everyone, including me, thought that I had a bad head wound. A field dressing was applied, I refused the offer of morphine, Holden retained the wheel, probably with some relief, and off we went back down the divisional centre line to find the field dressing station.

When we arrived there, I had blood all over the front of my battledress, as well as on my face and hands, probably because I kept trying to find out if I was really badly wounded or not. Strangely I didn't feel ill, just rather dazed, but already I had the beginnings of a monumental headache. On arrival I was laid out on a stretcher, visited by our brigade padre, a dear old Benedictine monk, and rushed into a tent. Initial examination showed the extent of my fraud. It was mainly blood and little wound. Seven stitches and a few minutes later I emerged walking, quite recovered, to be greeted by a bewildered Benedictine who admitted that he had been preparing to give me the last rites. Like the doctor, he told me how very lucky I had been. They thought that it was probably a mortar fragment, but it could have been a stone thrown up by the blast from a Panzer- faust or a mine. Anyway, I wasn't unduly put out by it, and felt rather heroic and proud of my bandaged head, as well as my well-bloodied battledress.

When we arrived back at the echelon, now established in a large orchard outside Bayeux, I handed over the map and the orders to Titch and then went back to the jeep where Holden had very kindly laid out my bedding roll under the trees in the dappled shade. I remember washing in my canvas bucket before stretching out on the bed and then, complete amnesia. I think that I had been given some pills which must have helped, as when I awoke, although I still had a headache it was not a very bad one. I was ordered to rest that day. To my annoyance I discovered that I had lost my signet ring. I imagine that it must have come off when I was washing and I had emptied it out with the water on to the grass. I searched diligently but failed to find it. I often wonder if some local farmer discovered it later.

There was an amusing sequel to this episode which

occurred on the arrival of C Squadron, who had just landed direct from England. Titch sent me to collect their echelon and bring it along to our position. I went, bloody bandage, green and gold side hat and all. I found them lined up on the divisional centre line just the other side of Bayeux. I reported to Henry Huth, who was as busy and laconic as ever and didn't even comment on my state, to my chagrin. However, one of his young officers standing on top of his tank, saw me, blanched and exclaimed 'My God, Bill, are there snipers about?' I shouted out 'Yes!' and to my delight, on went his tin hat and he shot down into his turret. I must have looked very piratical.

I returned to the echelon, and the next day, handed the troop over to Bob Butterfield. When the actual moment came, I found that I was reluctant to part with this, my first command. It was amazing how close we had all become in so short a time. I loaded my few belongings on to Titch's jeep and he then drove me down to La Butte to take over 3 Troop in A Squadron. I felt very nervous and I wondered how they would react to my youth and inexperience. However, I was determined to do well and to show that I knew my stuff.

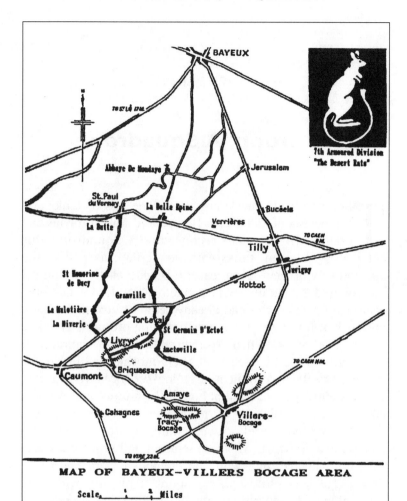

MAP OF BAYEUX—VILLERS BOCAGE AREA

Scale, ½ 1 2 Miles

It is impossible on a map of this scale to include the network of minor roads
which connect the farms-hamlets-villages and towns. There was a veritable
spiders web of tracks and narrow lanes. Most of these were bordered by high
banks, topped by thick hedges. These not only prevented the tanks from turning
once committed but also brought visibility for the crews down to virtually nil.

47

THREE

3 Troop, A Squadron

The battle at Granville crossroads, the loss of tanks and the deaths of Bill Talbot-Hervey and Mike Browne had created the need to reconstruct A Squadron. This entailed replacement tanks with new crews, as well as the appointment of new troop leaders. Despite all the training I had received, taking my own troop into action for the first time against an enemy who had already demonstrated their ability and their will to fight was a very daunting prospect. The new members of my troop had experienced the loss of comrades in battle already, and I felt that their morale would not be improved by the appointment of an inexperienced troop leader. I was twenty years old and although the gunner and wireless operator in my tank were of a similar age, the driver and co-driver were older and so were many of the rest of the replacement crewmen. My troop sergeant, Bill Pritchard, was a solid and capable man who had previous experience in the desert. He was philosophical about it all and was very welcoming and supportive to me. We became close friends over the ensuing months and developed great respect for each other. It was he who told me that I came to the troop with a good reputation and that, provided I didn't try to be too brave but used my head, then he had no doubt that I would make a good troop leader. I took the advice in the spirit in which it was meant and resolved to temper my desire to 'do well' with a strong dose of prudence.

My troop corporal, Alan Howard, had been drafted in from Bill Talbot-Hervey's troop and was not too pleased to find himself with yet another schoolboy. He seemed to be much older than I was, but in the event, as I got to know him, I found that there was only a couple of years between us. He was a staunch ally to have in the troop and although he always kept a certain distance, we both got on well together and saw eye to eye on the way things should be done.

The introduction to my new troop took place in a muddy field in the pouring rain. My crew were all huddled together under a leaking tarpaulin, which was propped up on some rails, borrowed from an adjacent fence. It was very cold despite the time of year, and they had their blankets wrapped around them. Luckily for me it was Allen, the gunner's, birthday and his friend Smith, the wireless operator, known to his crewmates as 'Don't talk Pith Smith' because of his lisp, fancied himself as a cook and had created a special birthday cake for him. It was made out of crushed biscuits and ration chocolate and bore a lighted cigarette instead of a candle. As he couldn't blow it out, it was passed round as a form of ceremonial smoke. The cake was duly cut and consumed with relish, accompanied by a mug of tea. It was somewhat heavy, but tasted excellent. After about half an hour, I began to suffer agonising stomach twinges to the extent that I eventually had to 'run for it'. I had no sooner established myself, in the rain, athwart the pole stretched over a longish trench which served as our communal lavatory, when Allen appeared, equally doubled up, quickly followed by other crew members, plus Sgt Pritchard, who suggested that Smith ought to patent the mixture after the war. Smith kept a very low profile that evening. After such an eventful start it was relatively easy to be on fairly intimate terms with them all.

Piff Threlfall, my squadron leader, had fought throughout the desert campaign with great distinction, and been awarded a Military Cross. To me he was a demi-god, totally unflappable and always prepared to listen. In common with the rest of the squadron, I trusted him implicitly and was quite prepared to risk my life for him if he should demand it. When we received our orders on that evening in June, he made sure that I fully understood my task and then told me that he would have no worries about MY area. I left that 'O' Group positively exuding confidence.

The squadron had the task of guarding the left flank of the division, facing the villages of Granville and St-Germain-d'Ectot. I was to be the left-hand troop of three and was to site myself overlooking the valley which separated the two forces. I had to get as far forward as I could without disclosing my presence to the enemy. My secondary role was that of covering the road which ran from Bayeux to Villers-Bocage. I was backed up at this point by another troop commanded by Dallas Barnes, which was sited about 400 yards behind me.

I slept well that night and was surprised when I was roused and told that it was 0330hrs and time to get organised for the day. We packed our kit on to the tanks, mounted, and at the signal started up. Tanks are noisy creatures and the roar of their engines, the popping of their governors, the transmission whine and the clatter of tracks as we moved off, made me feel that the enemy for miles around must realise that we were coming. We followed the squadron down the track for about fifteen minutes, and then I turned off to the left with my troop, following a new track which had been marked out with white tape by the sappers. This brought us through the gun-lines and to the forward infantry positions. It was still dark. The infanteers were all stirring and manning their trenches ready for the first light. The false dawn was showing as we growled past the last of their outposts and swung south-east across the fields, heading for the top of the ridge.

I have always been very confident about my map reading but I was nervous this time, and very relieved when I hit the high point of the ridge exactly as planned. I was also delighted to find that the small indentation that had been indicated on my map actually existed. I had decided to place the three tanks against the rear of the hedge-topped earth banks if at all possible, and we did this just as the first signs of dawn appeared. I adopted a triangular formation with my tank about 200 yards to the west of the road, Sgt Pritchard some 100 yards to my rear and Cpl Howard in the same hedge, but on my right, about 75 yards away. I placed two men on guard in each tank while the rest put up the camouflage. By these means, two tanks covered the main road and at the same time, two had an excellent field of fire over the ground to our front.

The sun was well up by this time, and we had a splendid view over the valley. We watched and waited. This was the moment when an enemy would be likely to appear if they had detected our presence or if they were mounting an attack in our area. As the visibility improved, so we began to see enemy movement on the opposite hillsides. The noise of tracked vehicles was clear in the early morning air and there was a frenzy of activity in some woodland below the ridge, which was slightly hidden from us by trees. There was no movement close to us, although I had a long discussion with Allen about a possible infantry position which I thought I detected some 400 yards to our left front, astride the road.

By 0700hrs, as there seemed to be no immediate threat, I stood the troop down and we brewed up, not in our usual quick way by throwing half a gallon of petrol on earth contained in a half petrol can, but on our stoves. I could not risk any black smoke, nothing gives one's position away more quickly. We all ate a gargantuan breakfast, including the usual cold M&V, which comprises tinned meat and vegetables. It is wonderful what an appetite you have when you are young and living out of doors in perfect weather. It gains added zest from the exhilaration of shared risk and companionship.

With the initial problems behind me, I began to relax and to feel more at ease with the crew, while they in turn responded by talking more freely and joking together. It was the continuing development of the relationship which deepened as the days passed. I was very fortunate in having such a friendly, competent and supportive bunch of chaps. After breakfast I visited both of the other tanks and exchanged information as to procedures, areas of responsibility etc. Not being on watch, I then sat down comfortably beside the tank, with my back against the bank and basked in the sunshine which was pouring through the hedge.

I suppose I must have dozed off, as I suddenly became aware of the noise of engines. Thinking that this must be enemy to our front, I shouted a warning and leapt up on to the back of my tank. As I stood there I realised that the sound was coming from behind me and turning, I saw two British armoured cars racing towards us. They were coming down the Villers-Bocage road from the direction of Dallas Barnes' troop, i.e. from our left rear. When I first spotted them, they were heading straight for the brow of the hill and the enemy lines. I waved my hat frantically, trying to attract their attention, but they were closed down and evidently concentrating on the road ahead. Suddenly there was a very loud bang and the front car stopped dead in the middle of the road while the second vehicle, a lightly armoured Humber reconnaissance car, slewed over to the right and stopped on the grass verge by the hedge. It was all over in a fraction of a second and I looked in stunned silence as smoke billowed out of the foremost vehicle. The enemy gun, probably a 75mm anti-tank gun, had been well sited to cover the crest of the hill and although we heard the crack as it fired we could only hazard as to its exact location. We sent this information back to squadron HQ and, putting the troop on full alert, I asked Bill Pritchard to give me cover from his tank while I went over to the two cars to see if there were any survivors.

I took my pistol and a couple of smoke grenades with me and working my way along the hedge reached the road. There was no sign of movement, the sun blazed down and I was surrounded by all the lovely soporific sounds of summer in the country. I remember once again experiencing that feeling that it was all a dream and that I was watching myself doing something, rather than actually being directly involved. I decided to inspect the rear car first as it was closer to the hedge, so I crawled down the grass verge until I was level with it. The front fascia panel had been ripped open, and the armour piercing shot had made its exit through the near side, leaving a gaping hole. I pulled myself along on my stomach, arriving midway along the side of the car and then, taking my courage in both hands, gradually stood up and leaning over the front of the bonnet, peered through the driver's visor which had remained open. The interior if the vehicle was a shambles, the driver and the gunner must have died instantly and there was no question as to their being alive. As my eyes became accustomed to the light in the interior of the vehicle, I saw the commander, a young corporal, lying against the rear bulkhead. His eyes were open and he stared back at me without moving. I remember whispering to him, 'Are you all right?' I had a sort of creepy feeling that the German infantry were all around me. To my astonishment he shouted something and, insofar as it was possible to do so in so confined a space, leapt to his feet, shot out of the turret, and dashed back down the road towards our own lines. I found out later that he was wounded in the arm and chest, and that the shock of the sudden death and destruction around him had deprived him, temporarily, of the power of movement.

I felt a little more confident at this point as nobody had shot at me, and having regained the cover of the hedge, indicated to Bill Pritchard that I would now have a look at the front vehicle, which was directly on the brow of the hill. Working my way along the ditch I arrived level with it. It lay, slewed across the middle of the road, in full view of whoever had fired that shot. I called out asking if there was anyone alive and there was no reply. I confess that I felt very frightened at this stage, I suspected that there were wounded men in the vehicle, but was acutely aware that to get to it required me to cross the road in front of the enemy, then to climb on to the turret, open the hatch and help any wounded to escape. At the same time I knew that I was being watched with interest by my troop. It was then that I remembered that there was a small escape door built into the left-hand underside of the Humber armoured car. The hull of this vehicle was hexagonal, which provided deflective surfaces to help reduce the chances of shots penetrating its sides. The bottom of the hull sloped inwards and it was on that slope that the door had been sited. I slid along on my stomach to the point where the grass verge met the road, eased out one of my smoke grenades and threw it towards the front of the car. Luck was on my side and a dense cloud of smoke billowed up covering the car from direct view. I jumped to my feet, ran round the back and squatted down against the hull on the far side. There was no door catch but the door was ajar and as I touched it, it swung fully open. The dismembered body of the gunner slithered out of the aperture. I felt terribly sick and filled with horror at this very personal contact with violent death. However, my fear that someone would fire at this sign of activity goaded me on, and I dragged his body out on to the road and thrust my head and shoulders into the aperture. The driver had been killed by the armour piercing shot, but the commander, a

54

sergeant, although wounded, was alive but wedged between the side of the turret and the 37mm gun mounting. He was unable to move, as the shot had struck the side of the breech mechanism, forcing the mounting to one side, and the deflector plate was pinning him against the wireless set. Overcoming my revulsion, I pulled myself up into the turret and gradually, with his uncomplaining help, eased him round the breech and on to the floor. I doubt that it took more than a couple of minutes, but it seemed like hours to me. He was bleeding heavily from his left leg and thigh but, showing great stoicism, insisted that we got out of the vehicle before I tried to dress his wounds. I half dragged him out of the narrow exit, and laid him down under the vehicle, it must have been agony for him. Then, throwing caution to the winds and in full view of the enemy, we staggered to the hedgerow.

Alan Howard was there with one of the troop. They supported the sergeant to the shelter of the tank, gave him morphine and administered some temporary first aid. We then awaited the arrival of the doctor, who had been alerted by Bill Pritchard. I smelt of death. My tanksuit was covered in blood and horror, and once the exhilaration of the rescue had worn off, I felt desperately sick. My crew made me sit

down, brought me some water to wash in and plied me with tea and kindness.

Youth is incredibly resilient and within a short space of time all that I could remember was the excitement and the pleasure of achieving the rescue. I forgot about the bodies lying in the two cars, I suppose that I was full of pride and adrenalin. In a short time the medical half-track arrived with its conspicuous red crosses on the side and removed the casualty. I was not best pleased with the medical orderly as he drove straight over the field to my tank, thus showing the enemy exactly where we were. I was pretty terse with him about this, my newfound authority adding strength to my annoyance, and he left somewhat chastened, driving around the hedgerows.

As soon as the half-track was out of sight, I returned to my tank and, kneeling on the engine covers, leant over the back of the turret casing. It was to become my favourite position during the weeks ahead. I found it comfortable and capable of being sustained for long periods of time. It enabled me to cover the ground in front with my binoculars while I steadied myself with my two elbows firmly lodged on the turret top. Smith remained in the tank looking through the gun sight and listening to the wireless. There was no wind, all was quiet and it was very hot, even in the shade of the thick hedgerow. One sensed the presence of the enemy rather than seeing much of them and I think that, instinctively, we imagined them to be sharing our feelings of lethargy. Movement was taking place, but as far as we could see only by German wheeled vehicles, which dashed along the road on the far side of the valley. In any event they were well out of range and we reported their presence back to squadron, more as a gesture to show that we were alert than in the belief that the information would be of much value.

On one occasion, however, there appeared to be a concentration of enemy in one of the woods on the far side of the valley, which we reported. Evidently this confirmed other reports, as we were informed that American guns would give the area some attention. Shortly afterwards there was the most frightful eruption in and around the woods, as literally tons of shells landed with great accuracy in the area. Apparently, the American guns were temporarily short of a good target and we were told that a corps of artillery was used, mainly composed of 105mm gun-howitzers. It was a fantastic 'stonk' and must have caused havoc.

Allen, my gunner, who was off duty, had just started to organise the lunch when suddenly the peace was shattered by a stick of mortar bombs which fell close to us along the front of the hedge. They made a series of frightful bangs, and stupidly, instead of slipping into the turret, I jumped off the back of the tank and joined Allen among the cooking pots. I arrived there all in a heap, just as the second stick fell, this time in the hedgerow itself. Shrapnel struck the tank and whined about in a most threatening fashion. We pressed our bodies even more tightly to the ground and hoped that it would miss us. I was acutely aware that the third stick, logically, would fall directly on us where we lay. It was a very uncomfortable few seconds as we tensed up waiting its arrival. There was a total silence, not a movement, no voices and no bombs. After what seemed like an eternity, we got up with relief and scrambled, somewhat belatedly, into the tank. We then sat and watched our front to see if the enemy who had pinpointed our position with such accuracy was preparing to attack. However, nothing further happened and I had just given permission for the crew to dismount again, when Bill Pritchard warned me over the troop intercom that the colonel was approaching accompanied by some brass.

I jumped down off the tank and saw Colonel Cuthie a few yards away, he had crossed the field diagonally, exactly as the medical orderly had done, but on foot; Brig Hinde was with him. I saluted and before I could stop myself, launched into a tirade about the thoughtlessness of people who crossed open fields and disclosed the positions of those who remain there. I was starting to warm to my theme, concerning those who were left there to take whatever the enemy decided to throw at them, when Colonel Cuthie raised his hand and said quietly, 'That's enough.' It was a gross impertinence on my part, but to their credit neither of them showed any irritation and looking back on it, they must have realised that it was sheer nerves. Colonel Cuthie then said that he would remember my point, while the brigadier, with a huge smile, congratulated me on my camouflage.

By this time the other members of my crew had dismounted and were standing by the tank grinning at each other as he spoke. He then asked me to recount the story of the two armoured cars, which he said came from 61st Recce Regiment, had seen no previous action and were just out from England. Finally, we mounted the tank and I showed them the general situation on my front. He and the colonel studied the ground for some minutes through their glasses before jumping down and wishing us goodbye. Again that smiling comment on my splendid camouflage and they left, walking down the hedgerow, to visit Alan Howard's tank before rejoining their scout-car at the rear of the field and driving off. It was then that Chamberlain produced the mirror and invited me to look at myself. My face was covered in smuts and grease from the cooking pots among which I had lain when I had tried to shelter from the mortar bombs. This, combined with my green and gold tent hat, made me look like a badly made up seaside minstrel. I was not very amused.

A couple of minutes later mortar bombs burst around Cpl Howard's tank and we had barely managed to clamber into ours when all hell was let loose around us as well. I felt somewhat justified in my recent outburst and hoped that the colonel heard my report over the W/T. Although such mortar attacks were not particularly dangerous if one was inside the tank, it was obvious that the enemy had us under close surveillance, and that undermined the feeling of security which we had enjoyed before.

Hunger is one of the best cures for caution, and I am sure that more people have been killed or wounded during the war because they wanted food or water than for almost any other reason. We were no different from all the others in this respect and as soon as it seemed reasonably safe to get out of the tanks we did so and started eating our belated lunch. We had been lucky with the ration packs this time and had procured an 'E' pack. This was the troop favourite and it included a delicious treacle duff, I ate half a tin of this concoction with great pleasure. I allowed the spirit stoves to be lit so that we could brew some tea but the remainder of the food was cold. It was obvious that we were being watched and I felt that one man out of each vehicle at a time was enough. The sweltering heat continued throughout the long afternoon and it was difficult to stay alert. The enemy were certainly both cunning and well trained, as although we knew they were nearby, we saw no movement whatsoever except in the far distance.

I found that my binocular vision was becoming blurred, so I handed over duty watch to Smith and left my tank to pay a short visit to the other two. This had the additional benefit of resting my eyes from the continual glare of the sunlight intensified by the binoculars. I made sure that I walked along close to the hedge, spent some time with Alan Howard and his crew and then, leaving them, slipped through the undergrowth to the bank behind us where Bill Pritchard's tank was hidden. He was in great form, they had brewed up under the cover of a large hole in the bank and had made themselves very comfortable. They had not been mortared either, so they had the laugh on the rest of the troop. While I was there he remarked how clearly our voices carried back to them and suggested that this was a point that we ought to watch in the future, as it gave away our positions just as easily as a sighting would. I sat with him for several minutes and was about to leave, when I saw Allen get out of the turret of my tank. At the same time I heard someone shout something, although I was certain that Allen wasn't addressing anyone. I then realised that the voice was actually coming from the road and not from the tank. Bill Pritchard had also heard the voice and had come to the same conclusion as I had. He grabbed the 'B' set microphone, told my crew to mount and close down quickly. Allen, obviously called by Smith, jumped on to the back of the tank and slid out of sight.

It was a matter of seconds before the mortar bombs landed all around the tank and I had a prime view of my own crew under fire. While this was going on we were both searching the road for signs of life, and then it all fell into place. The enemy had infiltrated up the road as far as the foremost armoured car of the two that they knocked out earlier in the day. They had sited an OP with a wireless set or telephone somewhere in the hedge on the left-hand side of the road, and they were watching us from under the lee of the car itself, protected from the sight of anyone looking from the height of the turret of a tank. I was anxious not to disclose Bill Pritchard's position, but this was the only tank which could fire at the spot where we both agreed that the OP must be. He shared my desire to protect his camouflage, and he suggested that I remained with his tank while he made his way along the bank and tried to pinpoint the exact location of the enemy post. The idea was that if he could so direct the fire as to knock them out with the first shell, then they would not be able to report from whence it had been fired. When he returned he was delighted, as he had seen movement and reported that there were at least two soldiers in the ditch on the road side of the hedge and he felt confident that he could shoot close enough to their position to either destroy them or force them to move. I left matters to him, got out of the tank and settled myself in the bank some yards away to the right. He fired three high explosive shells in quick succession with a long burst of Besa (turret machine-gun) for good measure. I then rejoined him on the turret to await developments. The shots had been right on target and we thought that we could see a grey figure lying in the ditch. I stayed with Bill for another few minutes and then, as there appeared to be no further movement and no sound of their wireless, I made my way back to my own tank with great caution.

It was about 1600hrs by this time and we settled down to the interminable wait for last light and our recall. As the next couple of hours passed, so did our feeling of being overlooked by the enemy, and gradually the tension relaxed. The crew members who were not on watch got out of the tank and sat against the bank smoking and talking, and we drank endless cups of tea. There were visits from members of the other crews and the corporate troop spirit began to build. It had not been a bad day so far, we had come under fire and survived, we managed to get the tanks to the right place, had helped the wounded from the armoured cars and secretly, I think the men were pleased that I had launched forth in a tirade at Colonel Cuthie and the brigadier. Personally speaking, I was less happy about the latter point. We had a long discussion on the question of the evening meal and in the end, as a crew, we decided that we should not eat until we had reached harbour that night.

The afternoon passed into the evening and by about 2100hrs, as the light began to fail, we clambered back into the tanks and were very much on our guard. It was the first time that I had experienced that terrible feeling of vulnerability that one has in a tank turret. It is very high and thus seems visible to all for miles around. It is much more easy to see and to hear when one is actually on the ground, and I became increasingly aware of a number of blind spots from which a clever enemy could approach to within very close range without being seen. I decided to place my tanks with more mutual cover next time.

The evening passed without any activity in our sector and at about 2200hrs the squadron was called in. Our three tanks started without difficulty and slowly we made our way back through the fields until we rejoined the divisional route which we had taken that morning. We were the last troop back and as the squadron sergeant-major allocated us our parking place I suddenly realised how desperately tired I had become. It was with the greatest difficulty that I helped to hand the jerrycans of petrol up on to the engine covers. Luckily we did not require ammunition and already had our rations so, while the crews put out the bivouacs and cooked the evening meal, I went over to see the squadron leader and to find out if we had any special orders for the next day. Piff Threlfall was standing up and eating his supper when I arrived, offered me a drink, and I stood there talking to him and to the squadron second in command, Bob Ames, as if I was an old hand. It was good for my morale and I began to feel much more a real part of things. A few days later, I received a note (overleaf) from Lieut-Colonel Brownrigg, officer commanding G1 Recce Regiment from which the two armoured cars came.

I received orders for the following day, much the same as before, but this time joining a company of the Queens and supporting them in a defensive role. I was just about to leave when Bob took me aside and said, 'If you want to get on in the regiment I would advise a little more tact when you talk to your colonel or any senior officer.' I was about to

O.C. A Sqn *informed* *office.*

Comd 8H

61 Recce Regt RAC,
BWEF.

30 Jun 44.

Very grateful -

Will you please pass on to 3 Tp "A" Sqn our thanks
for their rescue of wounded from two of our Armd Cs
which were K.O'd N of Granville on 26 Jun 44.

R. Abrowning

PHAB/CW.

Lt Col.

O.C. A Sqn:
Show to Lt Bellamy who may keep the letter
if he wishes to. *CR. 1 July 44*

apologise when he added, 'You were right in what you said,
but in future don't say it with such aggression and don't
choose senior officers to say it to.' That was the last I heard
of the matter, although Colonel Cuthie did call me Bill from
that day onwards!

I returned to the troop, heavy-eyed but happy, collected
everyone together quickly, thanked them for their help
during the day and gave instructions for the morning. I then
went and sat on my blankets to eat my supper. That was the
last thing I remember until about 0330hrs, when I was
woken again as it was time to leave. My supper plate was
still by my side untouched. I was so hungry that I had no
difficulty in eating it standing up in the turret as we awaited
the signal to move off.

The story of this first day's experience as a troop leader is
representative of many days in actions of this kind in which
the regiment was involved. War is 90 per cent boredom and
10 per cent excitement. Luckily, human beings tend to
remember that which was exciting or pleasurable, and to

forget the dull days. It seemed to me that we were perpetually exhausted during those first days in Normandy. The nights were very short and the good weather made daylight last even longer than usual. I rarely had more than three to four hours in my blankets and eventually, when the weather permitted me to do so, I developed the habit of sleeping on the back of the tank with the gearbox cover open and my backside comfortably ensconced there in. I also developed great skill in catnapping at every possible opportunity, and as a result felt remarkably fit despite the abnormal hours.

This habit did lead to an embarrassing situation during 'Market Garden'. We had carried out a night move and had stopped in the early hours of the morning in a wide and open field. My troop were on guard duty and as we were all tired I felt that I must do my stint. Apparently, I was woken up, acknowledged, got out of my sleeping bag, and sat on the exhaust manifold with my feet tucked into the gearbox. I must have then gone straight to sleep and fallen gently backwards until my head was pointing towards the ground, down the back of the tank while my feet, hooked under the gearbox, prevented me from falling. The ubiquitous Alan Howard woke up, he was next on guard, apparently shouted, 'Bill's been shot,' and joined by several others rushed over to me. When they had unhooked me, they found me unwounded but asleep. They pulled my leg mercilessly. Alan, who was nothing if not direct, said, 'If you'd been a soldier found asleep on guard like that you'd have been court martialled and shot!'

One of the other problems caused by these conditions was that food that has been cooked very slowly on stoves or using petrol can cause fires, and often we were too tired to bother. However, with their usual ingenuity, tank crews developed a strap to hold a billycan, with its lid on, on to the grille which protected the exhaust pipe vents on the back of the engine covers. On being called into leaguer and having filled the billycans with water, we put in our selected tins for the evening meal, clamped on the lid and strapped them to the exhaust with wire. They were ready for eating by the time we arrived.

"Strap them to the exhaust"

FOUR

Battle in the Bocage

My second day's command was marred by a brutal death and by my misunderstanding of the location of the 5 RHA battery supporting us, which nearly cost a lot of lives.

All began well; we were on time and arrived at the right place, overlooking the Villers-Bocage approaches; met up with the Queens company commander and then deployed nicely alongside their forward positions under some trees, with our noses about ten yards back from the a stone wall. The only snag was that beyond the wall was a lot of undergrowth stretching for about one hundred and fifty yards and leading to a wood which ran away to our left. Also connected to it was a long thin but dense thicket which sloped away down the hill to our right for about a quarter of a mile. I asked the company commander if some of the infantry could cross the wall and take up their positions on the far side, while we protected their right flank. He refused, quite rightly from his point of view, because, as he said, his right flank was well protected anyway. Nevertheless, I felt vulnerable to the potential stealthy approach of enemy infantry through the undergrowth. However, there was no other shelter available to me, so I grouped the three tanks together within an area of about 100 yards and had two men on watch in each turret.

The Platoon Commander sited his section headquarters near the front of my tank. He was rather stuffy about having tanks with him, saying that they drew fire and that his men had to suffer while we sat in shelter. I felt that this was a repeat of my own fears of the previous day, and didn't react.

Once again it was a wonderfully warm sunny day, everything was silent, the woodland was full of birdsong, and butterflies flitted about on the bracken. Smith was on lookout with me when he quietly nudged my arm, indicating that I should look to my near right. I could hardly believe my eyes. There, on the other side of the wall but within 50 yards of my tank, was a three-man Panzerfaust crew with a *feldwebel* in charge of them. The two soldiers were older men but the *feldwebel* was young, deeply tanned and very much in charge, clearly directing their movements through the undergrowth. The colour of their greenish-grey uniforms and the red edging around their epaulettes seemed to be etched against the back-cloth of the greens of the scrub around them. In fact the whole episode still stands out in my mind in real 'technicolor' detail. They were searching for us, bending low so as not to be seen over the top of the wall, but for some extraordinary reason although they appeared to be looking straight at us, the camouflage, plus the fact that the sun was behind us, must have prevented them from spotting us. They stopped at a track junction and, because of the waist-high bracken fern, were themselves completely invisible to our infantry. They had not been spotted by either of my other two tanks, probably for the same reason. What was even more frustrating was the fact that my gunner was unable to get a sight on them as they were just too close to the wall, which totally blocked his view. As they stood there, peering in our direction, I made a mental note never to take up a supporting position again without the gunner having a field of fire.

I called down quietly to the platoon commander, who at that moment was standing just by the front of my tank, asking him to lend me a Bren gun or his Sten gun so that I could fire at them. He flatly refused saying that such weapons as he had, he needed, and walked away from the tank towards the left but behind the wall. Meanwhile, Alan Howard, who was in the right-hand tank, and on a slight rise in the ground, had spotted some movement but couldn't determine if it was the Queens or some enemy. He came up on the 'B' set and asked if it was enemy and whether he should fire his turret machine gun. I think that the sound of this call, crackling out over my headphones, disclosed our whereabouts to the Germans, as the man with the Panzerfaust lifted it on to the shoulder of the second man and pointed it in our direction. I shouted over the wireless for Corporal Howard to fire, and at the same time fired at them with my pistol, although they were really out of range unless one was very lucky or very skilled. I think that I had fired about twenty rounds in my life and all those on a range under clinical conditions, so I certainly wasn't the latter. At the same moment the Panzerfaust was fired, and I actually saw it in flight. It went about 5 yards to the left of my tank, hitting the parapet of the stone wall at exactly the spot where the young officer from the Queens was walking. It decapitated him as if by surgery, and his body seemed to continue on its way for a few paces before falling. It was revolting and totally unexpected. It distracted me for a few vital seconds and, although I heard the sound of Alan Howard's tank firing, when I looked back to the woodland I could not see any sign of the three Germans. It was all over in a couple of minutes but it remains as one of my most vivid memories of the war.

I reported this event back to squadron who instructed to switch me to another frequency and to direct some 25-pdr fire from 5 RHA on to the woodland ahead. I had done this several times in training but this was my first attempt under war conditions. The object was to give the gunners the map reference of the target with such accuracy that they hit it first time. If, as is often the case, the reference given or their calculation of range or line was slightly out, then you applied correctives, up or down, by adjusting their shots by eye. I made contact, warned the infantry sergeant what I was doing and gave the gunners the reference. In a remarkably short time the shells whistled overhead and landed with great accuracy but a little to my left. 'Right two hundred,' I said, over the wireless, giving the correction.

There was a short silence and then the most appalling whine and a bang as the next shot landed right on my troop. I shouted, 'Stop firing,' over the wireless and seconds later Bill Pritchard arrived on the back of my tank plus map board. 'For God's sake can't you read a f——g map, sir?' he shouted. 'That should have been UP 200 not right.' I realised that I had assumed that, as is the case on a range, the gunners are always sited behind you. You cannot assume this in war, as sometimes, map-wise, the guns are actually ahead of your position. In this case, the guns were sited to our left front, because we were part of a redoubt. After all this excitement, the day settled down once more to routine, but I had learned another lesson which was to stand us in good stead later on. Luckily, no one was hurt as a result of my error.

The ensuing days and weeks were composed of patrols of this nature, and although it would be wrong to say that each one of them produced such moments of excitement, it was true that each day brought a fair measure of challenge and of humour. The regiment was heavily engaged in patrol activity in countryside that was totally unsuited to tank warfare. These were the days of the real 'Bocage' fighting. As we advanced through the country, we could rarely see further ahead than the hedge of the field in which we were. Once we were in position we could often see across a valley or get a reasonable field of fire, but it was difficult to find such places without having the disadvantage of adjacent cover, which enabled enemy infantry to approach without being detected. Equally it was difficult to keep in touch with the tank troops on your flanks and 'friendly fire' was a constant hazard. Instinctively, if you saw enemy you fired and, in the heat of the moment, it was difficult to remember that the adjacent field was, possibly, occupied by someone else from your squadron. The early morning task of getting into position for the day's patrol was always hazardous.

Dust thrown up by the tracks presented us with an additional problem as our front mudguards had been ripped away by the dense hedgerows, and the dust and grit always seemed to blow into our eyes. This was especially bad for the driver and co-driver, as they were actually sitting between the tracks, peering out through small round apertures which funnelled the dust stream into the tank. By the end of the day we were all filthy, mouths full of grit and eyes raw. Conjunctivitis was prevalent, more especially among those who 'lived downstairs'. Despite that, the problem was mild at this time compared to the dust which we experienced later in the July battles. I was unable to wear goggles, as that prevented me from using my field glasses, yet it was vital to keep a close eye on every quarter. I can't remember any operation during which I had my head inside the turret, it was always out and I kept my two turret lids open, using one on either side to give me some protection.

When the sun shone, it seemed to glare down on us from dawn to dusk and, although this had its pleasant side, it was a great disadvantage when one had to keep alert. On a number of occasions, I developed a type of binocular blindness and found it impossible to see with any clarity. Luckily my crew members were keen and competent, and helped by taking over the watch duties when I felt my vision deteriorating.

Dust clouds, too, were always a great giveaway to tank movement, while the noise and smoke from the tank engines was another problem. I went to some lengths with the squadron fitters to ensure that my tanks, at least, were running on a mixture that didn't create all that smoke on starting up, which was the hallmark of the Cromwell. The twin exhausts pointed skywards and the smoke went some twenty feet into the sky. Very soon, we became experts in finding our way through the narrow lanes and the tricky small fields. A fund of experience was built up in a matter of a few days and we became both battle-trained and hardened in a way that had become impossible to envisage while we were still in England. I felt a growing confidence in my ability to handle the troop under all conditions and with this confidence came the determination to see that no member of MY troop should be killed. This in no way meant that we would become over-cautious or try to escape from all danger but that, whatever the circumstances, I would use the ground to advantage and not expose tanks to unnecessary risks.

During this time I received my first batch of letters from Audrey and, oddly enough, at the same time I found among my kit the china doll which had stood on her dressing table and which she had given to me (or had I begged it?) before we left England. She, the doll, was to be my mascot. The troop adopted her without question and, by the informed, my tank named 'Abbot of Chantry' became known as 'Little Audrey, Abbess of Chantry'. This small white china doll, which I still possess, was dressed in her bouffant ball gown, and attached firmly to the top of the searchlight which fitted on to the right-hand side of the turret. She stayed there until I changed vehicles during January 1945. She became a very strong symbol of good luck and survival to the whole troop. During one of the battles in Holland my tank crashed through a thick hedge and, unseen by me, she was knocked off her perch by a branch. I was immediately notified of her loss by Bill Pritchard who was following me. It was a moment when we, as a troop, were reforming at the front of the hedge and then dashing forward in line to the next obstacle, covered by our new Challenger tank. As I was about to give the signal to move, I saw Sgt Pritchard leap out of his tank, he rushed back to the hedgerow, picked up Audrey, clambered on to the back of my tank, handed her to me and shouted, 'I'm not going without her!' I knew that she had become a very much-loved mascot, but until that moment I hadn't realised the full extent of her role!

Despite the frequency of the patrol activities, there were a number of days when the squadron was resting or when my troop was in reserve. These were the days when we carried out our routine maintenance, checked the more readily available bits of the tanks, tried to develop better ways of storing our ammunition and generally attempted to remedy any inherent defects. We also slept. This was a technique mastered by the whole of the British Army and they could all sleep anywhere at the drop of a hat. Between these activities we washed our clothes, and ate the most imaginative meals concocted from the very excellent rations with which we were provided. Normally one ate as a crew, but sometimes we all got together and had a troop feast. Local provisions were scarce but there was an occasional chicken and there were crews who fed well on the fresh meat obtained locally from cattle killed in the shelling. I was not an enthusiast. Local wines were scarce but there was a good supply of Calvados. It was rather raw for my young throat but very acceptable to the older and more experienced members.

My great friend and fellow troop leader, Tony Hind, demonstrated the power of this fiery fluid one day when he developed agonising toothache. Luckily it was a rest day and his troop was sited in a hedgerow alongside mine. He had obtained some aspirin and other pills designed to mitigate the pain, but nothing was being very effective. The driver of the squadron ARV (armoured recovery vehicle) was a man of great resource, a skilled 'discoverer' of local produce, and Tony was one of his favourite officers. Hearing of his discomfort, he came along and offered him a mug of Calvados. 'Wash it round your mouth, sir,' he proposed, 'you'll find it better than all those medicines.' Tony did as he suggested, at first, with care, taking small ladylike sips and emptying the first mug slowly. A second mug was provided, as the treatment was proving beneficial, and he emptied this second mugful with remarkable speed. However, all that this achieved was an intensification of his thirst and despite my protestations a third mug was provided. He didn't manage to drink much of this as, although by now he had lost his toothache, he was drunk as a lord. His troop sergeant and I had the greatest difficulty in restraining him from dancing off around the leaguer, singing and shouting. Eventually, the drink and the sun put him to sleep so that, to our relief, peace reigned.

Poor Tony, he woke up a few hours later, not only with raging toothache but also with a terrible head. I borrowed the squadron jeep and took him back towards the beachhead to find the dentist. They discovered an abscess under one of his teeth and I sat at the mouth of the tent while the dental officer took the offending tooth out and drained the cavity. Most impressive, I thought, to sit in the sunshine and have a tooth extracted. Tony didn't see it in quite the same light.

A few miles to the east and along the road from our position, the Panzer-Lehr Division of the German army was putting up a very stout defence of the village of Hottot. The area of this village was the target for our artillery and we used to sit, transfixed, and watch the thousands of shells, set to 'air-burst', which were sent in their direction. These shells, by some technical wizardry, burst in the air over the target. The result was that the shrapnel flew in all directions and must have been most unpleasant for the unfortunate soldiery on the receiving end. The guns responsible for this were 3.7 ack-ack guns and they were sited in a field about 200 yards behind us. These guns went off with a particular 'CRACK' which was very distinctive and really hurt one's eardrums. After half an hour of them in action we would have preferred to be out on a patrol.

One particular night they seemed to fire incessantly and we enjoyed very little sleep. At dawn, I was sitting on the ground leaning up against Bill Pritchard's tank, talking as we drank our early morning cup of tea and idly watched the co-driver of my tank, Tpr 'Goldie', emerge from his seat in his usual leisurely fashion. Suddenly a look of horror came over his face and giving a great shout of, 'Look out,' he plunged to the ground off the side of the tank. Before we had time to react to this warning, we were astonished to see a huge red tubular object emerge from the co-driver's hatch. It rose slowly, silently and ponderously to a height of about 10 feet before crashing to the ground. Thank goodness it fell to the front of the tank and into an open space. It was the compressed air cylinder, which somehow or other had become detached from its clamps and, venting, had emerged like an Apollo rocket, chasing Goldie out with scant ceremony. He treated it with considerable respect in the future. We had experienced some fast and bumpy cross-country driving during the evening of the previous day, so this had probably loosened it from the clamps.

One of our favourite pursuits was to eavesdrop on other squadron wireless nets while they were active and we were resting. This could be very exciting and, on occasion, very amusing. One splendid moment occurred when C Squadron were out on a standing patrol and Michael Payne, a young and popular troop leader, was in a hedgerow with shelling taking place to his front. Apparently the whole area was covered with cattle, who paid little attention to the lethal objects dropping around them and concentrated on the job in hand. Suddenly over the air came the laconic voice of Micky, 'Gunner, you see that poor cow in front which has just been wounded? Put the poor devil out of its misery will you?' He obviously imagined that he was talking on his intercom and not broadcasting to the world, because he then remained on the air with his microphone switch pressed. There was a moment of silence and then the rat-tat-tat of the Besa machine-gun. Then came Micky's agonised cry, 'Not that one you bloody fool, the one on the left!' We didn't let him forget that for a long time.

One day while we were on patrol a massive bombing raid took place, and the stream of Lancaster bombers roaring overhead seemed endless. They did not fly at a great height on these daylight raids and we could see them clearly. I believe that on this occasion, the main targets were in the area of Caen, but a lot of activity occurred over Villers-Bocage which was to our front. In fact, the village appeared to be the pivot point around which they turned as they went back towards England having completed their mission. We saw several bombers shot down by the heavy ack-ack fire from the German 88mm guns. These dual-purpose guns were the bane of our lives too, because their armour piercing shot could penetrate any tank armour plate with frightening ease. However on this occasion it was not our worry, but we felt for the unfortunate bomber crews who could not seek any cover and had to fly steadily in column through it all. It gave the German gunners the perfect opportunity to get accurate range and direction and it must have seemed like a pheasant shoot to them.

Suddenly, not far in front of us, a Lancaster exploded in mid-air and broke into two pieces, the forward section with the wings and the engines hurtling to the ground, and the tail section, which appeared to be intact, falling comparatively slowly, and see-sawing down like a falling leaf. Eventually it crashed into a field some 400 yards to our right front. I asked permission from squadron HQ to go out and see if there were any survivors but was told that the matter was already in hand. So we waited with some impatience to see what happened. Soon a C Squadron scout-car appeared with a body strapped on to its engine covers. It was the rear-gunner, who was very much alive but who was thought to have a broken back. We were told he reached the base hospital safely and, after such an astonishing escape from death, we all hoped that he made a full recovery.

We had experienced wet weather and storms during the early days of the invasion but most of the time it had been warm and sunny. However, June ended with a lot of wet weather and July continued this trend, so that we were always moving in thick glutinous mud. This made the simple business of living so much more difficult. It was impossible to clean your boots properly when you climbed up into into the tank, so the mud came with you and you spread it liberally around the equipment. It got into the bedding because, as we huddled together for shelter under the waterproof covers, we couldn't help treading on other people's beds in our efforts to reach our own. Cooking became a dreaded chore and nothing ever seemed free from wet or filth.

The tracks on my tank had stretched during the past weeks and we had to take a link out in order to shorten them. This was not a major operation in normal conditions but could cause problems if the track pins wouldn't knock out or the track adjuster had seized. In the event all went well and we heaved on the rope attached to the end of the track, pulling it over the idler rollers on to the adjuster wheel at the front of the tank. The drill then was to start the engine and run it very slowly with the track up on the sprocket, until it was taut and capable of being rejoined by replacing the track pin. Unfortunately, Chamberlain didn't see my signal to stop, and the whole tank ran forward off the track which was then neatly laid out behind us in about a foot of mud. We then had to manoeuvre a second tank into the morass in order to tow the tank back on to its own track. Tempers became a little heated despite the rain. We were unrecognisable at the end of this little exercise and although we were suffering from an excess of water it was difficult to find enough to wash in.

Early in July, we handed over our sector to another

division in order to prepare for a new operation east of Caen, so we were withdrawn to the area known as Jerusalem Crossroads. The mud was fresher there. One of the major cross-country tank routes ran west from Jerusalem Crossroads to Abbaye Mondaye. It turned due south just before the wall of the abbey in a wide arc. The whole route was marked out by white tapes. A young German soldier had been killed at this corner while taking part in the defence of the abbey. He lay feet first by the actual tank turning point and was gradually being cut to pieces by the tanks as they slewed round. On the night in question, being in convoy, I couldn't stop to move him, so I ordered my driver to swing wide so that we didn't touch him. I still feel a sense of revulsion and of sacrilege about him lying there, and find it hard to get out of my mind.

The weather started to improve and we spent our days training with 131 Brigade in the art of infantry–tank cooperation. Most of them disliked tanks, considering them to be noisy, smelly, absolute giveaways to their positions, and a large target which drew enemy fire. Despite this we got on very well together, and forged a degree of understanding which was to prove very valuable in the months ahead.

During the period of our stay at Jerusalem, we set up a squadron Officers' Mess and brought the mess 3-tonner up from the echelon. It was of great benefit to us all, as, under relaxed conditions, we had time to exchange ideas, experiences and discuss problems. We entertained other officers from the regiment and also from different units in the brigade. I made a number of very good friends during this time, such as Geoffrey Armitage and Alfie Burns from 5 RHA and a number of platoon officers in the 1 RB (Rifle Brigade). We remained in touch throughout the campaign and were often in the same battle group. It made things so much easier when you knew your fellow combatants as friends and not just names.

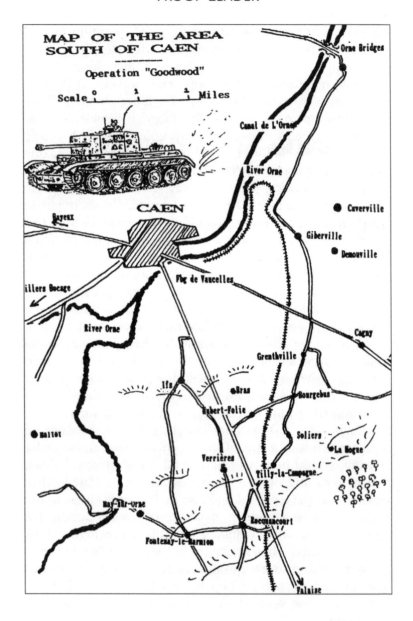

MAP OF THE AREA
SOUTH OF CAEN

Operation "Goodwood"

Scale 0 1 2 Miles

CAEN

Bayeux

illers Bocage

River Orne

Haltot

Orne Bridges

Canal de L'Orne

River Orne

Caverville

Giberville

Demouville

Fbg de Vaucelles

Cagny

Grenthville

Ifs

Bras

Bourgebus

Hubert-Folie

Soliers

La Hogue

Verrières

Tilly-la-Campagne

May-sur-Orne

Fontenay-le-Marmion

Rocquancourt

Falaise

FIVE

Battle of Caen Plains – Operation Goodwood

At the end of the second week in July we were told by Piff Threlfall that there was to be an armoured breakout battle south of Caen. All the British armoured divisions would be involved and, hopefully, it could presage the end of the fighting in the Bocage. It was an attractive prospect to us all, as none of us relished the idea of more of the 'close' fighting that we had experienced during June. The code name for this operation was to be 'Operation Goodwood'.

During the next few days divisional units moved from their existing harbour areas and together with the 11th and the Guards Armoured Divisions assembled on the flat open ground north-west of Caen. It must have made a wonderful target from the air as there were well over a thousand tanks concentrated in a relatively small area, and it was fortunate that the German air force lacked the facilities to attack in strength during the daylight hours. However, there was evidence of their reconnaissance aircraft, so we knew that we were expected. Our own area for concentration was east of Bayeux, near a village called Brécy. There was no cover to be had and we were drawn up in long lines, two abreast, by squadrons.

Colonel Cuthie called an 'O' Group, which was held in a small field containing a few apple trees. He had assembled all ranks of the regiment, it was very cold and we crowded together as he outlined the plans for the attack. A large-scale map had been prepared showing the whole of the beachhead, this was displayed on the front of a 15-cwt truck. Using the map as the key, he gave us a most detailed account of the objectives and of the part we were expected to play in the forthcoming battle. In common with my fellow troop leaders, I felt very optimistic about the outcome, although Colonel Cuthie stressed in his talk that the country was very open, with long rolling hills, and as such it would be relatively easy to defend, offering good fields of fire as well as excellent visibility. As to the opposition, it appeared that our old enemies, the three SS Panzer Divisions, were thought to be already in place and waiting. The younger members among us were all a little disappointed that the other two British armoured divisions were to go ahead of us, but this was to some extent compensated for by the fact that we were to be in the centre and were to be driving south towards open country. Morale was very high.

The order to move came on 18 July and during that afternoon we started off on the long approach march, aiming to arrive at the bridge over the River Orne, north of Caen, at nightfall. The initial moves went well and we made good progress, but as we got within a few miles of the river, so the traffic ground to a halt and we sat in our own dust and fumes, growing more and more impatient. As darkness fell, we heard German bombers overhead and then the sound of exploding bombs, which we presumed were aimed at the bridges. We all became very bored by the delay, and our enthusiasm for the bridges declined a little as the noises of bombs became louder. The greatest problem however, as we approached the river, was the appearance of thousands of vicious little mosquitoes. These drove us mad with irritation as there was no way in which we could escape them. They got into the turret and poor Allen, the red-haired gunner, who had so little room to move down there and couldn't see the insects anyway, was writhing with bites. I had the bright idea of wetting a rag in petrol and wiping this over our faces and the backs of our hands but even this didn't have much effect. It did, however, stop the 'downstairs' half of the crew from smoking, which caused further ructions and I think, increased the ferocity of the mosquito attacks. I definitely lost face over this. Happily my co-driver, Goldsworthy, had a fund of stories and limericks, and he regaled us with a selection of these which helped to pass away the time. This was the first time that I had heard anyone sing the full, twenty-four verse, unexpurgated version of the 'Ram of Derbyshire'. Not, however, the last.

During this period of waiting we were moving forward in fits and starts. Suddenly, to my surprise, we arrived at the top of a small hill and saw the river below us, clearly outlined by the light of the night sky. The approach track was marked out in the usual way by white tape, and this wound down the side of the hill in a gentle 'S' shape. There was a line of trees slightly below us to our right and at the end of these was the bridge itself. By this time the bombing, which was fairly accurate, had been intensified and the whole of the bridge was lit up by flares. Our actual descent was made at a snail's pace as there was terrific congestion on the far bank and, despite everyone's desire to get on, there was no way of 'jumping the queue'. In common with everyone, I felt that the whole of the German air command was watching me – personally. However, the bridge remained undamaged and we negotiated it without difficulty. I was very impressed to see the Airborne divisional troops on duty there. They were very calm, were acting as police and waved us on as our turn came. I felt that they had every right to feel a little proprietorial about the bridge as, after all, they had captured that area and I presumed were responsible for erecting it.

Before we had made much progress on the other bank, we were halted again and told to stand by. We snatched what sleep we could, remaining in our tanks, and moving on from time to time through the small villages, most of which had been destroyed in the fighting. I remember that there were occasional sounds of enemy aircraft, but my over-riding impression is one of amazement at the strength of the bombing carried out by the Allied air forces. There seemed to be a continuous stream of bombers flying overhead and dropping their bombs to the south of us. This was accompanied by the biggest bombardment by the artillery that I had ever heard, and the whole effect was one of an irresistible force crushing the enemy ahead of us. How wrong I proved to be in making such a deduction; it is incredible how the human being survives this sort of attack and emerges unscathed with the same determination to continue the struggle. I recall somewhat later in the campaign a young SS soldier being shelled in his trench by a tank, but every time the bombard-ment ceased he emerged again with his Panzerfaust, determined to knock out the tank. Eventually the tank was driven along the side of the trench so that the tracks buried him. When he was extracted, muddy but unharmed, he was still as belligerent as ever.

Eventually the order came to harbour in a large open field near Demouville, where we lined up in squadrons, and dispersed as best we could against the shelling. It was not comfortable and, although the news which trickled through was of successes, the enforced inactivity was not good for any of us. It was with great relief that we were called to squadron Orders and ordered to prepare to go up to Fours, a village about two miles to the south of us and to support the 1/6th Queens. Unfortunately, in the event only one troop was required, so the rest of us 'sat it out' where we were. This was the first time that I experienced the terrifying arrival of clusters of mortar bombs which created a Stuka-like whining moan as they were fired and continued this noise until a few moments before landing and exploding. The bombs landed in a tight group and were very effective. I was told that these mortars, called 'Nebelwurfers', were very dangerous to fire and that the Germans manned them with crews of Russians; I don't know whether this was true or not.

That evening the whole squadron moved up to Fours in order to act in a supporting role in the attack on Verrières, which was to be launched by the Canadians. In preparation for this, we sited ourselves in the ruins at the edges of the village. In the afternoon, before we were committed, the rain started again and became incessant, turning the whole area into a 1914–18 War muddy morass. It was unbelievable, there was no place to dry off, bedding was saturated and life very uncomfortable indeed. We all began to think of our previous discomfort at Jerusalem with a sort of nostalgic homesickness.

The heavy rain prevented the armour from continuing to attack and the whole of Operation Goodwood splashed and spluttered to a wet and unpleasant halt. Shelling and mortaring increased rather than eased during this period, which, in turn, meant that we had to spend more time in our tanks. We were all cold and miserable. After a couple of days of this, with no actual attack by the enemy and no movement by us, we were withdrawn two miles back to Grentheville while B Squadron took over our role.

Grentheville was a hamlet situated alongside the railway line running south-west out of Caen. At the point where we were, this line was the major feature of the battlefield, as it ran along the top of a high embankment and we were unable to see over the top of it from our tank turrets. However, just next to us, there was a narrow tunnel under it, presumably for farm vehicles and cattle. We were told that the Guards Armoured Division were fighting in the area of Cagny, which was to the east of us but on the other side of the railway line, and the squadron was ordered to make contact to ensure that no gap existed. Bob Ames, who was the squadron second-in-command, took me with him in his jeep, and we set off at first light splashing through the muddy track under the bridge.

When we arrived at Cagny we found ourselves in a different world. The battle there was still in full swing, there were shells flying about in all directions and we had some difficulty in finding the regimental HQ tank of, I believe, the Welsh Guards. When we did, Bob reported to their adjutant while I waited in the jeep. Over all the other noises, I suddenly became very aware of the growl of low-flying aircraft and straight ahead of me, very low, and flying in a tight formation appeared eight German aircraft. They looked large and threatening, flying four up four back with lines of rockets hanging under their wings. They were camouflaged in brown-yellow and green and the whole scene, which must have been over in seconds, seemed to unroll slowly like a film. They were over us before we could react in any way and, without firing a shot, roared straight over our heads in the direction of Demouville and presumably, the bridges.

Contact having been established satisfactorily with the Guards Division, we returned to the squadron where we found that the shelling was just as bad in our so-called rear areas. During the evening of the following day, Alan Brodie was killed by a shell. He was one of the replacement troop leaders in A Squadron, and another friend of my own age. Later during the same evening, 24 July, we were told that we were to take part in an attack with the 1/7th Queens with the objective of capturing Tilly-la-Campagne. This was good news as we felt that at last we were going to get going, leaving the passive role of sitting and waiting for the next shell to burst. In the event I saw nothing of the battle as we were never committed, and that evening, under more or less continuous shelling, we turned off west again and the squadron was drawn up in two lines, one behind the other, on a slight reverse slope near the village of Ifs, just to the south of Caen.

By this time the rain had stopped and it was a warm damp evening with a cloudy sky. At about six o'clock, I was talking to Jack (Flash) Chapman, the squadron second captain, when a couple of Brengun carriers, manned by the Northumberland Fusiliers, dashed up and started to line up two heavy machine guns. I had never seen these heavy 0.5 inch guns before and was fascinated by the belt feed etc. Jack knew them well and told me that they were used a great deal during the Desert campaign. We were watching their preparations with interest, when we were joined by the squadron leader, Piff Threlfall. Their troop officer explained that the main arterial road ran south-eastwards there and they were going to fire straight down that, to deter would-be German troop movement. They fired for about ten minutes on a fixed line in the general direction of Tilly and when they had finished they scuttled away. Jack remarked that we would now reap the benefits of their visit by increased shelling, and the three of us walked back to the tanks together. We then stood behind Piff's tank, talking, laughing and generally enjoying Jack's fearsome reminiscences of soldiering before the war when he was a trooper in the regiment.

My tank was sited directly behind Piff's and Jack was next to me, on my right. Everyone was in their tanks, except for the three of us, as there was still a bit of shelling going on although it was not very close. Piff was smoking his inevitable pipe, I can't picture him without one, sitting on the ground with his back against his tank, map-board on knee and his very discoloured and worn old 8th Hussar green and gold side hat perched on the top of his head. Suddenly the shellfire came much closer and both Jack and I, feeling a little foolish, made for the shelter of our tank turrets. Piff, unperturbed, sat there quietly smoking. The next salvo fell directly to the front of his tank and as I watched him from the top of my turret, he fell quietly over on to his side. Evidently, the shell splinters had passed under the tank and hit him in the back. Both Jack and I jumped down from our tanks and rushed to pick him up, both hoping that he was stunned or lightly wounded; but he had been killed outright and we were left, two grown men, unashamedly weeping in front of any of the squadron who cared to look. He was the most wonderful man to have as a squadron leader, unflappable, experienced, a good counsellor and a friend to all of us. We all loved him and although we had other good squadron leaders, those who had been privileged to serve under him never forgot him. Bob Ames, the squadron second-in-command, took temporary command of the squadron.

The next day was grey and miserable but fortunately we had plenty to do, as the regiment was ordered to support 131 Brigade and we were told to dig in and occupy defensive positions. The shelling and bombing continued all day and night. Few of us managed to sleep, and most of those who did had to do so inside their tanks or in a slit trench. I was fairly lucky as we managed to dig a trench in

dryish ground and the tank was parked directly alongside it, between us and the enemy. We slept in that, huddled together under a waterproof cover. Some of the crews had thought to dig trenches and then run the tank over the top as a shelter but I had been told that in another regiment one of the crews did this and the tank then settled in the mud, slowly asphyxiating them. This story dissuaded our people from trying it, and personally speaking, I never had any further desire to get under the tank whatever the conditions outside.

At first light on 27 July the squadron was ordered to support the 1/6th Queens in the area of Verrières again. I was told to proceed to a position on their left flank looking out towards Bourguébus. I motored on, expecting to pass through the lines of the infantry trenches but, somehow, in the semi-darkness, I overran them and eventually, seeing a troop of Cromwell tanks deployed up ahead, decided that I must have misread my map. I had a quick word with Bill Pritchard, and drove on towards them with the intention of stopping and asking them what the form was. They were drawn up in line ahead on the forward lip of a small indentation at the top of the hill. As I approached them I became somewhat apprehensive because nobody turned round to look at us although there were two men standing in the turret top of the centre tank. I decided that it would be wise to halt the troop in the slight cover offered by the dip in the ground, and proceed on foot. So, getting out of my tank, I ran across and clambered up on to the engine covers, noticing as I reached it that the tank was marked with the red maple leaf on a white background, which indicated that it came from one of the Canadian brigades. I scrambled along the side and was about to tap one of the occupants on the shoulder when I saw that they were both dead and that the tank had been knocked out, probably some days earlier. The other two tanks were also burnt out.

I returned to my own tank rather shaken, just as the first of a number of 88-mm shots roared low over the top of us, coming from the direction of some woods towards La Hogue and Garcelles. One ricocheted off one of the dead tanks in front of us. We certainly got the message, they knew where we were. At the same time, in the growing light, I saw some infantry in trenches about half a mile away to our right rear and I realised that I had overshot my proper position, and was on the left of the 1/6th Queens but well ahead of them. It was pretty clear that, at least until dark, I had no hope of getting my troop out of the shelter that we were in without sustaining casualties. I reported on the wireless to squadron HQ, told them that we were pinned down but safe and that, despite this, we had an excellent view of the distant woods. Already, we were beginning to identify some armour moving there and had seen a Tiger tank as well as other unidentified tanks, armoured personnel carriers and lorries. Bob Ames confirmed our new position with regimental HQ and told us to stay put and report. It seemed that by good luck we had selected a better observation point than the one to which we had been directed.

The three tanks of my troop were still sited in a triangle exactly as we had stopped on arrival, with Sgt Pritchard's 15 yards to my left rear and Cpl Howard's directly behind me and some 50 yards away. The nearest of the three knocked-out tanks was about 100 yards to our left front. By this time it was broad daylight, the sun was out and we were all feeling very hungry. Owing to the indentation which concealed us, the turret crews were unable to see anything except the ground immediately in front of their tanks and I called over to Bill Pritchard that if they wanted to, they could dismount and brew up. He had to clamber on to the roof of his turret in order to let the others out, and immediately the firing began again with shells landed unpleasantly close to us. It was obvious that we were well in the sights of the enemy and that we were not going to be allowed to enjoy our day. Eventually, the co-drivers slipped out of their side hatches and having grabbed the necessary rations, set up the cookers on the nearside mudguards and brewed up, still sitting in the shelter of their co-drivers hatch. Food was thus prepared on the 'Lower Deck' and passed up to us.

Meanwhile the situation to our front was becoming very exciting with plenty of enemy movement to report. There were a number of sorties by Typhoons during the earlier part of the day. The battle lines were so ill-defined that some errors of identification had been made by the air force, so I took the precaution of laying out the red air identification strip across the front of my tank so as to warn the Typhoon pilots that we were friendly. I did not fancy a British onslaught as well.

The day passed very slowly. The temperature, and the tempers of the crews confined to the tanks, became more heated as the sun rose higher in the sky. It was difficult to make life interesting to those members whose vision was restricted to a view of the reverse slope in front of us. I changed the two turret crew members over every hour or so, a massive manoeuvre as they had to squeeze through the small space behind the driver's seat but it was still very boring for them. To add to our problems we all needed to relieve ourselves from time to time and although the time-honoured custom of the empty shell case was adequate for most needs, there were greater problems which did not lend themselves to performances in so small a container.

Allen, my gunner, had endured problems of this nature for most of the morning and by early afternoon he could contain himself no longer. He shouted to me that he had to get out of the turret and whatever I said or did wouldn't stop him. I realised that he was at the end of this tether and as we had no shelling for some time, thought that there would be little risk. I began to ease myself out of the hatch and was about to slide out and roll back on to the engine covers, when I heard the noise of Nebelwurfers firing. Some instinct made me shout, 'Get Back,' and I thrust my feet down on to his emerging shoulders and we both tumbled in a painful heap, back into the turret. At the same time, Bill Pritchard's driver, Sharpe, who was watching from his driving seat, seeing me diving back, slammed shut the aperture port in front of him. Simultaneously, there was the most tremendous crash, our tank leapt into the air and there followed a series of huge explosions. We lay there totally stunned and deafened, heads singing and wondering what had happened. The 'B' Set crackled and Alan Howard's voice came on asking if we were all right. Smith replied that he thought so and we started to get ourselves untangled and reorientated.

The first thing that I noticed when my head emerged from the turret top was that the engine covers had been blown off the back of our tank and were lying on the ground some yards to our rear. Two of them were very badly buckled. The second was that the whole of the camouflage netting and the items stowed on the front of Bill Pritchard's tank had been blown away. A quick check showed that nobody was hurt, Allen had developed constipation and the real problem was Sharpe, who although grateful for my intuitive shout, was infuriated by the loss of four tins of biscuits which were stowed on the front of his tank and which he had intended for barter. It seemed that a batch of Nebelwurfer bombs had landed plumb in the centre of the troop area, at least one of them directly on the back of my tank and one on the front glacis plate of Bill Pritchard's. It gave us great confidence to see that they had caused so little damage. Curiously enough the blast must have gone upwards and not sideways as the bedding rolls, which were stowed along the mudguards adjacent to the engine covers, remained undamaged and were still in their places. Happily, this accurate mortar attack turned out to be the last time that we were on the receiving end that day and as dusk fell, we laid the buckled engine covers back on my tank and, one by one, we reversed out and returned without incident to the squadron harbour.

After a further night of shelling and bombing, it was almost a relief when the orders to move off were given next morning and we went back to a position some 600 yards to the rear of the one I had occupied the day before. The new position was fairly well sheltered but once again it had a good view over the German lines. It was another sunny warm day and the sky seemed to be full of Typhoons strafing the enemy positions. It was a fantastic sight to see them suddenly dip their noses and power down towards an unseen enemy. When they were some 2,000 feet up they released their rockets and often continued on down, firing their cannons as they went, before swooping up again and returning to their 'cab-rank' to be called to another target, or disappearing towards Caen as they went to reload for the next trip. I saw one direct hit on an enemy tank which exploded in a ball of fire, but there must have been many which were undetectable at so long a distance. On one occasion, a Typhoon was caught in the hail of shells from German anti-aircraft guns and we saw it catch fire as it dived. We waited to see the pilot eject but instead of that he continued, released all his rockets and with cannons firing, crashed into the forest, leaving a great plume of black smoke. They were very brave men and we were full of admiration for the way that they pressed home their attacks. Recently, I invited an old friend, Wing Commander Brian Spragg DFC, to lunch and we discussed the battle. He went back to his house, returning with his 'Pilot's Log'.

We were both in the same area for some of that time and he was probably one of the pilots of the very planes that we watched at work.

As the evening approached we had a coded warning over the squadron wireless that we were to move elsewhere. A little later we were called in, and at a hurried 'O' Group, Bob told us that we were leaving the area of Caen immediately and returning for another 'break out' battle near Bayeux. We were all exhausted by this time as it had been almost impossible to rest because of the rain, the shelling and the general activity. We were not allowed to spend the night sleeping, however, and in the early hours we commenced the long drive back towards our old hunting grounds.

It was the most incredible journey in a tank that I had ever experienced and seemed endless. We were allowed no lights from beginning to end, the route selected led us through parts of Caen itself, which was totally devastated, and, despite the almost superhuman efforts of the sappers, it was practically impossible in the dark to select the road from the rubble. As far as I could detect there were no buildings standing, the ruins had collapsed across the roadways and the roads were composed of the resultant piles of bricks, stones and general debris. Despite the torrential rain which we had endured, there was thick penetrating dust everywhere. To maintain visual contact, we were driving literally nose to tail until eventually, with great relief, we debouched on to a track running alongside the old highway from Caen to Bayeux. It was almost worse when the sun came up, as by that time we were well on our way in the area of Bretteville, and it shone straight into our eyes, blinding us with its brilliance.

My three tank drivers were magnificent, they refused to hand over to the co-drivers and stuck it out to the bitter end. I slept from time to time, standing where I was in the turret, with my elbows lodged in the turret-ring. I simply could not keep my eyes open and how the drivers managed to do so, I shall never know.

It was a relief to turn off west towards Condé-sur-Seulles and the old tank track which we knew would take us to Juaye-Mondaye, the centre of all our previous activities. We arrived at about 0800hrs, to be told that we would have to move again later in the day, must fill up and generally carry out all necessary maintenance. It was not a popular ruling; however, we all buckled to and it was amazing how quickly the squadron was back in a state of readiness. At the 'O' Group, which was called later that evening, Bob outlined the next operation to us, 'Operation Spring', which was designed to catch the Germans off balance by transferring the weight of the British armoured attack to the west of Caen. At the same time we heard more details of the American break-out from the Cherbourg Peninsula, it all seemed very exciting but really we were too tired to care. Thank goodness the move was called off, and we all slept like logs until well into the afternoon.

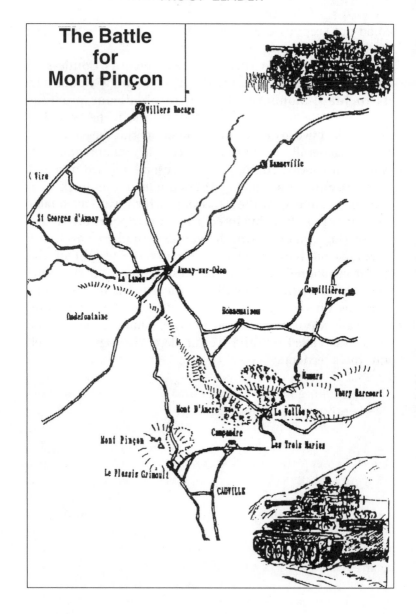

The Battle
for
Mont Pinçon

Battle of Mont Pinçon

On the evening of 31 July, we were told to be ready to move at first light, as the regiment was to take part in a divisional attack in the area of Aunay-sur-Odon, which was about 12 miles to the south of our position. The ultimate intention was the capture of the high ground called Mont Pinçon. This would prevent the Germans from reinforcing their forces fighting against the Americans, whose breakout from Cherbourg was making good progress, and would turn the flank of those defending the area south of Caen. It was to be an armour and an infantry battle, fought in fairly close country, but, we were told, the Mont Pinçon feature itself was good tank country.

There were delays during the early part of the day, but by mid-morning we were back on the tank tracks, and headed south through La Belle-Epine and St Honorine-la-Duchy, passing near the crossroads at Livry and the village of Bricquessard where the regiment had experienced so much bitter fighting earlier. Then the track was new to us; we passed Caumont, and ended our journey just after dark a few miles south of there, close to Aunay-sur-Odon at La Lande. It had been a long day again, especially for the drivers, and it had taken us over twelve hours of stopping and starting to do the 12–15 miles. Although there was no attack by enemy aircraft during this march, there was some bombing that night and our echelon was hit. The refuelling took place in the darkness and my old troop sergeant, Bob Butterfield, garrulous as ever, told me that he couldn't wait to have a cushy job back with a tank troop so as to have some more protection from the bombing. I think that he meant it too. I was sad to learn that one of my old troop, a driver and a good friend to me, Tpr Lawson, had been killed by the bombing at Caen and I began to realise how very lucky my troop had been so far.

We stood to at first light, but apparently the battle was hard and progress slow. B squadron was committed, but we stayed where we were, awaiting our turn. Luckily the weather was fine again, so most people took the opportunity to catch up on their sleep. The next day vindicated all the boredom, as we were dispatched to assist the 1/7th Queens in their task of clearing some woods between Aunay and Villers-Bocage. It was a copy-book operation, advancing with the infantry, holding as continuous a line as possible, and battling through the close-planted apple orchards and the thick hedges. Although it was not really anti-tank gun country, the danger was that we would fail to spot a German, concealed in the undergrowth, armed with a Panzerfaust. The difficulties were not only in remaining observant, but also in maintaining touch with the other two tanks in my troop, as well as the troop on either side of us and the accompanying infantry. This was further complicated by the need to prevent my head and shoulders, which were out of the turret, from being ripped to pieces in the trees and bushes.

My troop engaged no enemy, but I gained invaluable practice in controlling troop movement in close country, and we all improved our ability to work as a team under those conditions. We came back totally exhausted by the sheer physical battering that we had endured and were very content to bed down in defensive positions that night alongside the infantry battalion. Broadly speaking, the same situation continued for the next few days, and it wasn't until 7 August that Bob called us together and explained the plans for an attack by 22nd Armoured Brigade to capture Mont Pinçon the following day. The ultimate objective was a town called Condé-sur-Noireau which lay about ten miles to the south of us, while the more immediate one was Cauville, a village to the south-east of Mont Pinçon. The squadron was to advance three troops up and we were to lead the armoured column in our role as the divisional reconnaissance regiment. I was to have the left-hand troop and we were to advance at all speed.

It was the first time that I had felt any apprehension about an attack and how to handle it. Whether the briefing lacked conviction, or whether I just missed the comforting presence of Piff Threlfall I don't know, but I had a feeling of gloom about the day ahead which didn't leave me until we started to advance at first light on the morning of 8 August. Once we had passed through our own lines and were moving cautiously out across the fields into unknown country, I forgot all my fears and settled down to enjoy the challenge. It was a brilliantly sunny, warm day, the initial going was good and although we were able to report the occasional AP shot and saw vehicles at a distance, we didn't actually come up against organised resistance until about 0800hrs. Then Bill Pritchard, nosing through a hedge, was fired at by an anti-tank gun which, happily, missed him.

In the meantime however, all hell was let loose on our right and both the other troops in the squadron were reporting attacks, some of their tanks being knocked out. By this time we were still well to the north of Cauville, I wasn't yet in sight of the village itself, and the ground was rapidly becoming impossible for tank movement. It was real 'Bocage' with 2–4 feet high banks topped by thick hedges, interspersed with trees. Here again, many of the small fields contained orchards and the trees themselves were so low that often one couldn't pass beneath them but was forced to jink one's way through. This made it impossible for the gunner to see clearly and, as the tank commander was bobbing up and down in the turret, or trying to use the periscopes for sighting, it was all rather a nightmare. There was an added hazard for the gunner, who was sitting down below hunched over his gunsight, in a very cramped position. If he stretched his legs out through the turret cage in order to get some relief and this coincided with the gun hitting a tree while we were on the move, then the turret would have been forced round and off would come his legs. A chilling thought.

In the Cromwell tank it was difficult to remove shells from the racks and maintain a good rate of fire with the 75mm gun. The shells were all stored in bins round the turret floor, but as we were traversing all the time there were few opportunities for the loader to pick them up. In addition to this, they were about 2 feet 6 inches long and weighed over 10lb, so, as one had to load one-handed, they were unwieldy. It was our practice therefore, when we anticipated trouble, for the wireless operator, who doubled up as a loader, to sit with three or four shells across his knees, so that as we fired and the empty shell case ejected, he could reload in a matter of seconds. This was fine if one was static, but when one was bouncing about in all directions it became both very painful and extremely difficult.

By this time we had encountered a great deal of small arms fire, and I decided to call a halt while I reviewed the options open to us. The two leading tanks were hull-down behind the bank but we could see through the hedge top, and were engaging a number of enemy infantry moving about in front of us. I reported this to Bob and was told to try to probe forward again and see if it was possible to find any way round their position. I then asked Alan Howard, whose tank was in the hedge about 100 yards behind me, to try to break into the next field to his left and, when he had done that, to come up into line with us. He acknowledged my order, but, just as he was about to move, a number of enemy infantry dashed out from behind the bank on my left flank, at least one of them armed with a Panzerfaust. Neither Bill Pritchard nor I could fire at them immediately as we couldn't traverse our turret guns the requisite 90° owing to the density of the hedge itself. Luckily they had not realised that Alan Howard's tank was still sitting in the hedge behind, and as we two reversed out and started our traverse, he opened up with both machine guns and they dispersed, leaving a number of dead lying there. It was a nasty moment and I decided that we couldn't contend with an infantry attack unless we had some sort of a field of fire, so we all charged back through the hedge into more open ground.

Having gone back some 400 yards, I began once more to work the troop forward but this time, further out to the left (east). The whole area was alive with Germans and eventually, after a number of exchanges of small arms fire, we were told to stay put and observe, while artillery fire was concentrated in the area in front of us. The rest of the day passed in this game of Box and Cox, with shells thumping down into the German occupied areas while we moved from field to field taking the occasional pot shot and endeavouring both to watch closely and yet not be caught by an anti-tank weapon. We were called in well before last light, which was vital under conditions where one could be stalked by foot soldiers with such ease, and immediately assembled for an 'O' Group at which we were given new objectives for the following day. Once again, I was told to operate with my troop on the left flank of the advance.

When I returned to give the news to my two tank commanders, the three of us sat for a while smoking and talking as we looked out across the valley which sloped down from the harbour area. We could see in the soft, failing light the hillsides which contained the general line of tomorrow's advance, while to our right the grassy slopes of Mont Pinçon stood out clearly against the night sky. It was a hugely companionable moment during which, unspoken, we shared very real deep friendship.

We were ready to move off by dawn, and my troop was first to leave. I led them out in 'Abbot of Chantry', and in single file we slowly descended the road running down the hillside towards the woods and the brook with its narrow bridge at the bottom. It was a very still morning and there was no sign of activity anywhere in our area. Even the engines of the three tanks seemed muted, as the drivers avoided the giveaway of the dreadful banging of the exhausts, which always occurred with the Cromwell if they were driven on the governors or if they let the weight of the tank drive the engine. As we approached the bottom of the hill, I noticed a track running off diagonally to my left, which entered the wood and looked well used, I pointed it out to Bill Pritchard as an alternative route, but then decided that we must go straight on, as our orders were to clear the bridge as suitable for traffic. The bridge itself was not defended and there was no sign of mines. I eased over it, my other two tanks well back, and was relieved when I reached the slope on the other side without incident.

I then called the other two tanks over, reported the bridge clear and we went on cautiously, driving up the hill. The track became very narrow, running between high banks, and the concealment was perfect, only the tank commanders' heads being visible above the hedge tops. It was also an ideal place for an ambush and we had our Sten guns (acquired as a result of the previous problem) and hand grenades out on the turret lids. As we reached the brow of the first hill we spotted a well-entrenched German infantry position over to our right. We couldn't fire at them because our traverse was limited to the width of the hedgerows and they were out of effective Sten gun range. However, I was somewhat surprised to find that they took no notice of us. Bearing in mind that our instructions were to penetrate the enemy lines and reconnoitre, we carried on and I looked for a way of entering the fields of ripening corn, which were opening up on our left. We were unable to get into them by trying to climb the bank, as there was insufficient room to allow us to angle the tanks to do this. I suppose that if there had been a dire emergency, we would have tried but we would have probably torn off a track.

At this moment, I noticed that, ahead of us, although the track itself bore round to the right, a gap in the hedge led straight on into the corn. I indicated that we would take this and then form up in line against the right-hand hedgerow, before continuing our advance in the general direction of La Vallée. This achieved, we stopped for a few moments, and with engines idling, looked across the field. There was a hedge directly to our front about 300 yards away, and then apparently more corn as far as the eye could see in fields which were unusually large for Normandy. Beyond this and to our right was a small valley and on the other side of it, on the hillside of Mont d'Ancre facing us, and about three quarters of a mile away, a hamlet of perhaps ten houses. We were, as it were, looking into it and could see the church and, adjacent to it, a road junction and a small village green.

At first we could see no movement but as we studied the position with our glasses, we saw German troops in the village, walking about unconcernedly and loading up horse-drawn wagons. I reported this to squadron, and told them that I intended to proceed through the corn along the reverse slope of the ridge and see if we could identify more and decide what was happening. We set off in two-up formation, Bill Pritchard as usual on my left, with Alan Howard about 150 to 200 yards behind, and giving us cover. The corn came up to the level of our mudguards, it was almost ripe and I remember feeling a sense of desecration at its destruction.

We arrived at the next hedge, waited for Alan Howard to join us and then, in the same formation, set off again, moving up slightly on to the crest and concentrating on watching our right front, which was towards the village. Within about 150 yards of our leaving the hedge we crossed a field track running through the corn and then topping a slight rise, suddenly found ourselves in the midst of a company of German infantry. They were in sections of about ten men in file, carrying their arms, looking very cheerful and marching in two columns through the corn in the direction of the village. We were almost through them before we realised who they were and they took no notice of our two tanks whatsoever. Reflecting on it afterwards we concluded that, to infantry troops, one tank is very much like another and as we were not proceeding with stealth, they must have thought that we were part of the armoured group which were supporting them. At that moment Alan Howard's tank opened fire and as I turned my tank to allow my 'downstairs' machine gun to bear, so Allen opened up with the turret gun. The enemy disappeared as if by magic and although we raced through the corn firing, I doubt that we could have caused much damage except to their morale. Meanwhile Bill Pritchard had shot up the Kubelwagen (German jeep) which was following the infantry, and one of the two bodies in it was that of a young officer in the 326th Infantry Division. In the back of the jeep was a hammock and a Luger pistol, both of which I appropriated.

I realised that we must be behind the main German line and that these troops had probably just been relieved and were on their way to breakfast. We swung back towards our own lines, therefore, in order to try to re-establish contact and take the enemy from the rear but came under very heavy machine gun fire, so I turned back once more towards the ridge and the village so as to try to turn their flank. We reached the ridge, with my tank ahead of Bill Pritchard's by some 200 yards, while Alan Howard was to my right and stationary. I was concentrating on watching the area to my right front, where the enemy infantry had been, and Allen was searching through the turret telescope ready to fire if anything moved. Suddenly, I saw Alan Howard wave violently at us and at the same time his turret traversed sharply to the left. I looked across to my left and saw nothing and then looked up towards the village. There, standing exposed in the middle of the street at the road junction, was a German 75mm anti-tank gun, its crew around it, and its muzzle pointing directly at my tank. It all happened so quickly; as I instinctively gave the command to Allen, 'Traverse left 1000 yards anti tank gun. H.E. Fire on sight,' so there was the crack of Alan Howard's 75mm gun firing. The enemy gun seemed to explode and its crew fell or were blown in all directions. It was a fantastic shot and we all pounded the area for a few moments with high explosive shells to deter any further activity, I have no doubt that his prompt action saved the lives of my crew and me. We were all very grateful, although I could do no more than thank him on the 'B' Set at the time.

Instructions then came over the squadron net to exploit our position by moving back towards Mont Pinçon, and we were to try to establish contact with the other troops on our right. In view of the fact that we were obviously sandwiched between two layers of German defences, I decided to do this by crossing back over the ridge and, keeping below the skyline, return to join the original track and then review the situation. We saw no more enemy at close quarters and by mid-morning reached a large sloping grassy field, in the left-hand side of which was a small bushy quarry. I sent Bill Pritchard's tank on towards the quarry while we covered him from the hedge. There was no enemy response, and he reported that he could see over the ridge in front of him, had a good view of Mont Pinçon and could just see the village of Mont d'Ancre over to our left. I decided to settle there for a little while and give everyone a chance to relax and reorganise themselves, while we tried to pick up the movement of our own troops on the right.

We tucked ourselves well into the bushes, one tank facing the rear, and held a brief discussion with the two crew commanders as to what to do next. We were ahead of the other troops, we had an excellent all-round view and when I reported all this to Bob, he told us to stay there and report all movement. We stayed in or on the tanks at instant readiness, as we could hear the sounds of enemy activity all around us. There were enemy vehicles on the far side of the hill but all of them seeming to be moving towards the east. We saw sections of infantry marching, and from time to time German transport dashing about. We could have fired on them at long range but were instructed not to disclose our position but to remain watching and reporting unless we were the subject of a direct attack. It was very frustrating. We ate, drank quantities of tea, we reported, and as the long day wore on so my eyes became worse and worse owing to the bright light and the continual use of binoculars. In the end I had to give up and lie down on the engine covers and sleep while my crew kept watch. Everywhere was silent, there was no news coming over the squadron net and we turned the wireless down so low as to not give away our position. I didn't sleep for long but awoke refreshed and, as evening fell and the light changed, so my eyesight recovered.

At about 2100hrs, I requested permission to move closer to our own lines, but was told, rather brusquely, by Bob to stay where I was until ordered in. I was acutely aware at this time that there was enemy movement all around us and that it was increasing, yet without either going on foot, or moving one of the tanks, I couldn't see exactly what they were up to. I decided to stay put as we appeared to have remained undetected, and at 2200hrs radioed again to ask if I could move. Tony Hind answered and said that I was to stay where I was until Bob returned from an 'O' Group at regimental HQ. Tony was an old friend and I explained, fairly succinctly, what the problem was, but he couldn't override the orders which had been given to him, and I sat there fuming as darkness fell. Then we heard tank movement behind us and at the same time Bob came on the air to order me to return.

I had already decided that the bridge would be closed to us and probably mined. My plan was to cross the original track again, run down the middle of the field adjacent to that in which we had shot up the infantry, and aim to hit the trees to the right of the bridge, with the intention of joining the other end of the track which I had noted on the way out that morning. I ordered, 'single file and drive fast'. Nobody wanted to hang back and we went down the hill at a cracking pace, governors banging away, blue flames sprouting out of the exhausts and I have no doubt sparks as well, charging into the darkness. Just before we started up we were informed over the wireless that the tank noises were probably those of some Honey tanks, from the regimental recce troop which had also been called in.

By sheer good luck, the end of the track was exactly where I had predicted and we roared through the wood, splashed through the stream, and emerged to the accompaniment of assorted small arms fire. That night, on unrolling the bedding rolls, we discovered that they were full of holes. The three tanks of the recce troop came up the hill at the same time and we converged on the junction together. By this time it was so dark that they could only just be seen, and I was somewhat perturbed to find that I had to halt my troop in order to let them pass the gateway on to the track. I had my head out of the turret at this point and was shouting and waving to urge them on as it was an uncomfortable place to wait with all the German infantry around us. At that moment, I was horrified to see the turret of the rearmost Honey tank, which was about 25 yards in front of me, suddenly lit up by an intensely bright, blinding flash accompanied by a huge bang. Despite this, to my relief, the tank still went on, so we were able to get out on to the track and follow them up the hill until eventually we reached the harbour area.

As they stopped, I jumped down and rushed over to them to see what had happened. The tank commander, Sgt Webber, was desperately badly wounded and died almost immediately. As far as we could see, a Panzerfaust had been aimed at the tank and had ricocheted off the glacis plate before exploding against the open lid of the turret.

That was all I needed, my pent-up emotions burst and I went straight over to Bob and voiced my fury at his total lack of under-standing of the need to call troops in while they could still have a chance of seeing the mines or the enemy. I said a great deal more than I should have done and when he peremptorily ordered me to shut up and return to my troop, adding that I must be ready to leave to take up the same position the following morning, I just turned away and refused. It was all said in the heat, tension and anguish of the moment, but Bob reported me to the colonel immediately. Looking back on it, I realise that Bob was under great strain too, that he had carried out his orders and that I was totally strung up by the hours of isolation, and the waiting. However for me, the final straw had been the brutal death of Sgt Webber.

An experienced squadron leader would probably have interpreted his orders with more understanding and would have ensured that I had more wireless support during the course of the evening. If then I had returned as tense and as upset as I appeared to be, he would have left me to sleep it off, and in any event would have sent one of the reserve troops to carry out the task next day. Tony came along to see me later and suggested that I apologised. I agreed but, still piqued, said that I would do it in the morning. Despite all this, I slept, and when, at first light the next morning, the colonel himself appeared and came to my troop area accompanied by Bob, although very nervous as to the consequences of my refusal to carry out an order, I was more rational. I explained the situation to Colonel Cuthie, showed him the position that I had held and I apologised for creating such a scene. He accepted my apology as, very generously, did Bob, but gave me a very stern warning not to let my emotions run away with me ever again, reminding me that I had been too outspoken once before while under stress. He then called my troop together and thanked them for their efforts on the previous day, when apparently our information had been of the utmost value. Only one troop of the squadron was involved that day; they did not try to occupy the area where my troop had been, but they had the triumph of reaching the summit of Mont Pinçon without opposition. Bob was right and if I had gone I would have enjoyed that.

That evening, 10 August, the division was withdrawn, and the regiment sent to an area near Bricquessard to rest and prepare for the next battle. It was a pleasant place, the weather was fine and we all enjoyed the break. In company with a number of other officers I visited Bayeux, and managed a trip to the beachhead to see the great strides that had been made there since the landings. However, most of our time was spent in preparing the tanks for the next move. I took the opportunity of sending a Camembert cheese home to my mother. Apparently by the time it arrived it was in such a state of suppuration that the London postman besought her to instruct me never to send another. I understand that they had to bury it.

I remember that we were all very thrilled to be visited by the corps commander, General Horrocks, who talked to the senior ranks about the progress of the war to date and the tasks ahead. He came over to us as a very warm man, exuding confidence and determination, but one who cared for the welfare and safety of his troops. I think that he left us all feeling greatly heartened. It was the Feast of the Assumption, 15 August, and I attended Mass with as many Catholics as I could muster, in a cornfield. It was very hot at this time and it gave us an excellent opportunity to catch up on our washing. I pioneered a method of washing all one's clothes in neat petrol and then hanging them out to dry in the sun on the wire fence which ran alongside our area. This proved to be very efficient for exterior clothing but my underclothes were unwearable and gave me the most terrible rash. Later that day orders came through for the advance to the Seine.

SEVEN

The Breakout to Belgium

The 'O' Group of 15 August was one of the most exciting that I had attended. The colonel briefed us and told us of the progress being made in the tremendous battle that was being waged near Falaise. The two American armies, having burst out of the restraint of the beachhead, had swung west and were now south of the German Panzer and Seventh Armies. While, to the north, the Canadians, the Poles and other parts of the 2nd British Army had increased the pressure of their attack and were squeezing the Germans in a giant pincer movement. Our task, which was much to my liking, was to add to their problems by thrusting as fast as possible in the direction of the Seine and Belgium. Bob told us the detail of our own involvement, but at this stage there was little for us to do except prepare for the inevitable long and dusty drive across the whole of Normandy.

We set off in convoy on the morning of 16 August. As usual the start was delayed by the weight of the traffic, but we were under way by about 0900hrs. The total journey was only 20–25 miles, but the tracks were terrible and we took all day to reach our harbour area. It was baking hot, the dust was blinding and we were all very thirsty. However, it was a fascinating journey, as we were passing through the countryside which we had overlooked during 'Goodwood' and it was rewarding to see that it was now within our lines. The fields and roadside were littered with brewed up vehicles, and the villages looked like pictures taken in the First World War, in fact it was rare to see a building intact. I was particularly keen to see Rocquancourt which had featured a lot in my observations on the battlefield back in July. The village lay just to the north of our eventual harbour, and Bob gave Tony and me permission to drive up and have a closer look at it. It was of course completely flattened and we saw a number of German Mark Four tanks, as well as a Tiger and a Panther in the area, all of which had been knocked out, some of them by the Typhoon attacks which we had witnessed from our positions. These had usually had their turrets blown off or were in smithereens. Our harbour area was in a small hamlet, relatively untouched, called La Jalousie. An emotion that we certainly didn't share as far as that area was concerned.

Early next day we moved out through St-Pierre-sur-Dives, which was 12 miles to the east of us. We were given priority as the regiment, with C Squadron up, was leading the advance towards Livarot. We had some fun at St-Pierre itself, as the 51st Highland Division were there and we always got on well together. There was a great deal of leg pulling if the tanks were held up for a minute. Once when we stopped, a tiny little Jock appeared, bent under the weight of his company wireless set but in addition, slung across his back, was a huge goose. When Goldsworthy offered to relieve him of that problem, he shouted back that 'These f——g French hens were half the size of a good Scottish one', and he'd manage. Their divisional sign, the '51HD', with the front edge of the 'D' formed by the final leg of the 'H', was everywhere.

We were not committed that day, but both of the other squadrons, with their battle groups, were very heavily engaged, C Squadron most especially, and we were detailed to follow them with the role of backstop. I was listening on their squadron net while one of their troop leaders, who was a close friend of mine, Mike Young, was advancing down the road quite close to Livarot, and heard the exchanges when his troop was caught by anti-tank guns. Later we heard that he and a number of members of his troop had been killed.

Throughout the day squadrons of Spitfires had been flying overhead and had been machine-gunning just ahead of our troops. During the afternoon a rumour ran through the squadron that the colonel had been killed in one of these attacks, his jeep having been mistaken for a German one. This caused great consternation as he was a very popular and well-loved officer. Happily, someone at regimental HQ had the sense to come on the wireless and tell the squadrons that it was not true. Apparently the Spitfires, who had been foraging around looking for German vehicles to shoot up, had mistaken his jeep and some self-propelled guns of the Norfolk Yeomanry for an enemy column. The resultant machine-gun attack had been unpleasantly accurate, Tony Newman, the intelligence officer, who was driving him, had been seriously wounded and the jeep had crashed into the hedge. The Colonel, although badly shaken, was all right; we were all very relieved.

During the evening, C Squadron pulled back and we were briefed to take over the running for the next day, 19 August. My troop was sent to join Pat Hartwright of C Squadron for the night, and our orders were to lead off down the road towards Livarot in the morning. This was the same route on which Mike Young had been killed during the day. I found Pat well established in a farm on the north side of the road out of St-Marguerite-des-Viettes. It was a large prosperous set up and we made ourselves very comfortable in barns sited just below the crest of a small hill.

Pat and I talked for a long time that night, as he had experienced a great deal of action during the previous two days and knew the country ahead. He had been ordered to draw back from a small farmstead, where they had been well received earlier in the day, and was somewhat concerned about the farmer and his family who had remained there when he withdrew. At about 2200hrs while we were sitting outside in the failing light, we heard shots and shouts from the general direction of that farm. We discussed whether we should lead a patrol to investigate but decided that it would serve no useful purpose, so, anticipating trouble, we strengthened the pickets and stayed up late ourselves. The remainder of the night passed without incident. Later in the week I heard from Pat that the farmer and his family had been shot by German soldiers. In the regimental history it says:

> They [Henry Huth and party] went on with Captain Henri Belmont, the French liaison officer attached to the squadron, to the farm near where Hartwright had been with his troop on 18 August. It appeared that when Hartwright's troop arrived they were the first British troops to be seen and they were greeted with cries of 'Vive les Anglais!' and given eggs and butter and flowers. Some of the Germans had been watching this, and when the troops withdrew in the evening, four Germans went into the house and shot the farmer, his wife and two daughters and wounded another daughter and a boy of ten. We had this story from the daughter who had been wounded. The Germans, believing her to be dead, had left her. This only goes to show what foul creatures we were up against. The culprits were either 12 SS or 272 Fusilier Division. Even so there was no lack of French assistance.

Members of Pat's troop had told my chaps later that the boy had had his hands cut off and frankly, by this time, we were prepared to believe anything of the SS divisions who were totally ruthless.

Leaving Pat at first light, we drove carefully down the road towards Livarot. It was quite a major road with hedges on either side and visibility was good, compared with the Bocage. We were developing a new technique for this sort of country and tended to drive fast from corner to corner or feature to feature. Corporal Howard was lead tank and after a few miles I saw him beckoning me to join him as he reached a small rise. Drawing alongside him, in a hull down position, I saw two C Squadron tanks about 300 yards ahead of us. They had been knocked out and were lying across a ditch on the right-hand side of the road. Beyond them was a sharp left angled bend and the muzzle of an 88mm gun was pointing down the road through the hedgerow. Everything was silent and there was no sign of movement anywhere. We sat and watched for a few minutes and then I called Sgt Pritchard up to join me. I was convinced that the 88mm was knocked out, and I was not keen to fire our guns, as this only drew attention to us, but unnecessary delays were unacceptable as we were being urged by Bob to get on into Livarot.

In the end, I decided to risk it, and drove very fast down the hill, covered by my other two tanks. As I drew near to the two knocked out Cromwells, I saw Mike's body lying by the side of the road, together with the body of one of his crew. It was a lesson to me, as he was wearing one of the new tank suits with which we had been issued. They were made out of semi-waterproof material, but were a yellowish creamy colour and there was no way that the wearer could have taken cover without being easily visible. It was something which I had not thought of before, and I resolved not to wear mine in the future.

I took all this in as we powered on past them towards the corner, where to my relief I found the 88mm gun knocked out, with some of its crew dead around it. It was the one which Mike had destroyed. Clearly the position had been evacuated hastily, as they had not buried their own dead. I reported this to Bob and we went on down the road without meeting any opposition until we were within sight of Livarot itself, where we were fired on, but only by mortars. We could see a lot of movement in the town, but the bridge in front of us was blown, so we could not advance any further. We were ordered to stand fast, let the infantry catch up and then try to find a way round. Before we could do any of this, another troop of A Squadron found a small bridge intact further north.

Shortly after lunch we were ordered to leave our infantry friends and rejoin the squadron on the higher ground towards Lisieux. Almost simultaneously, the 1/6th Queens entered Livarot town itself without any major incident. We were somewhat jealous of them, as we could hear the bells ringing and all the noise of 'Liberation'. It looked as if they were enjoying a real party in a town which had not been fought over.

Having rejoined the squadron we were kept in reserve the next day, but on 21 August we were sent out to patrol the road leading to Lisieux. This was another good road but very exposed, as it ran for much of the way on high ground. The troop was located with some infantry and a gunner OP from 5 RHA in the area of St-Germain-de-Livet. At that time, Lisieux was held by a strong force of enemy as it was a key town on their major escape route. Our role was to watch, ensure that the Lisieux–Livarot road wasn't cut, and protect the OP whose guns were busy knocking hell out of the German columns passing through the town.

Later in the morning, we were ordered to find a way into Fervaques, which lay to the east of the main road. Strangely enough there was little opposition and from there, we were directed on towards Orbec, coming in from the northern side, where there were a number of dense woods and where the going, off the road, was bad. There was considerable opposition from both infantry and anti-tank guns. Tony and I were the two northernmost troops of the squadron and, when there was news that the road at St-Germain was threatened by an enemy force, were directed to get back there with all speed. In the event it proved to be a false alarm.

It was another warm and sunny day with a lot of white cloud about and, from where we sat in a hedgerow looking out over Lisieux some three miles away, I could see the sunlight shining on the Basilica of St Teresa, which was still in the course of construction. This dominated the town, and stood on the western side of it. It was built of a yellowish sandstone, which reflected all the light and gave the impression that it was illuminated. Below it, I could see dust and smoke from the shells raining down on Lisieux itself. The noise of the explosions was continuous and, from where we sat, the whole place looked to be devastated. I felt a sense of shame that I was participating in the destruction of a town which had housed so revered a saint as St Teresa. At that time, I knew very little about her life and her message, but I vowed that if I survived the war, then, as soon as possible after it was over, I would return and make a pilgrimage to Lisieux out of gratitude for my life. I fulfilled that vow in 1947. We stayed in this area for the ensuing few days. Eventually, when Lisieux itself fell, we were out to the east of the town. We were rejoined there by the regiment who picked us up as they went by and we all proceeded in style, through liberated territory, to a harbour area some five miles further east.

The next day, the squadron went into regimental reserve and we just followed along the centre line. It was a wonderful experience to be travelling through countryside relatively untouched by the war and populated by people who were deeply appreciative of the fact that they were now free of the German yoke. There were little knots of them by the roadside for much of the time and, personally speaking, I felt a sense of embarrassment at their joy and gratitude. They threw bunches of flowers on to the tanks, as well as fruit and vegetables. I cannot remember tomatoes at this stage but they became a fairly lethal compliment as we drew further north. A tomato at 20mph is a difficult object to avoid if you are sitting in the turret of a tank! And if it hit the front of the cupola, then it puréed and spread a long way. My schoolboy French came in very useful when we halted and I blessed my French master, Father Cedric, for his persistence in making us practise 'the spoken word'. We continued the advance, crossing the River Risle which ran north and emptied into the Seine near Honfleur. Eventually we found ourselves close to the outskirts of Rouen, and near to the Seine itself, at a village called Bouquetot. The division, which had done so well during the past weeks of fighting, was then pulled back to rest and maintain itself for two days.

On 29 August we were given the welcome order to prepare for the breakout into Belgium and Holland. This news was received by everyone with great pleasure. We had all suffered from the sense of restriction which the Bocage fighting had engendered. The move eastwards into Lisieux had been achieved slowly and at considerable cost, and the prospect of dashing forward, perhaps hundreds of miles into countries which up to now had seemed to be out of reach, was very pleasing. There was a lot of discussion about the war ending by the autumn, Berlin for Christmas or even, especially among the married members, home before Christmas. I shared these sentiments, although I imagined that the war would go on longer. I believed that we would fetch up against the Siegfried Line, and that a war of attrition would be battled out there before we actually captured Germany. My mind couldn't conceive the sort of situation which eventually developed.

We crossed the Seine at St-Pierre-du-Vauvray on 30 August. These bridge crossings were always frustrating, as delays occurred, traffic jams developed and senior officers waxed indignant if their own particular babies weren't

allowed over first. The problem that day was rain – soaking, blinding rain – which didn't help tempers; nor did it help the uncomfortable sappers, who were desperately trying to make a bridge out of the bits that the Germans had left, plus some pontoons and Major Bailey's ubiquitous portable bridge sections. Eventually, the rain stopped, the bridge was able to be negotiated and we crawled over it carefully. This time 'A' Squadron led the regiment along truly open roads, where the fleeing Germans had been the day before. We drove on through the cheering French for some forty miles and harboured for the night after liberating Gournay-en-Bray. It was a day in which we tasted victory, and I really began to feel that perhaps, after all, it was all over and that the enemy were on the run. How wrong can one be? I spent some time talking to an excited French couple that evening and although with my halting French it was difficult to understand the detail, their hatred for 'Les sales Boches' was pretty impressive, and I was happy to be British and a liberator.

I could hardly wait for the morning, because at orders that evening we had been challenged to get to the Somme the next day, to beat 11th Hussars, our armoured car regiment, to it and to capture the bridge intact. It was really thrilling stuff and there was no doubt that my enthusiasm was shared by the troop when I gave out the details to them later. We were in the lead on the right, with Tony Venner's troop, deadly rivals for the honour, out on our left, so the squadron was to advance in a two-up formation. We could choose our own detailed route, but the objective was to capture the bridge at Hangest-sur-Somme. This was a village about 12 miles north west of Amiens. The problem was the maps. These were poor prints of French maps and were very difficult to read; clearly the very speed of the advance had taken the ordnance by surprise.

We set off as soon as there was sufficient light to see by, and literally drove as fast as the roads could carry us. Perhaps at the very early stages we showed some caution, but as the day evolved and no opposition was encountered we grew in confidence and concentrated on getting ahead regardless. At one time I took to the fields, large corn fields with few hedges, and was delighted to find that, at that moment anyway, I was out ahead of the armoured cars which had been slowed down by the twisting roads. A little later, I was not clear where I was as I was out of contact with even my own squadron HQ, having totally outstripped everybody. I was forced to stop and ask an astonished Frenchman if this was the road to Amiens. I received an answer in the affirmative, a handful of apples all round and off we went again.

As we crossed one major road just to the north of Poiz, we spotted unidentified tanks to our right and assumed that they were part of the German retreating force. Sgt Pritchard stayed under cover by the side of the road acting as point tank, while Cpl Howard and I roared down the side of a wood, across the back of it and then burst out down the reverse side ready to tackle the enemy from the flank. Luckily before we fired, we saw that they were a very startled troop of Sherman tanks from one of the regiments in the 11th Armoured Division. It was a useful meeting as they were unaware as to how far we had advanced and this enabled them to carry on towards Amiens itself, which was their divisional objective, knowing that their northern flank was now covered.

One of the interesting things about this dash through France was the speed at which the news of impending liberation ran ahead of us. We were, without question, the first members of the British Army in the localities through which we passed, yet the French were out by the sides of the road as we arrived, shouting 'Vive les Alliés', and 'Vive les Anglais'. Good news, apparently, like bad, travels fast. I suppose, looking back at it, that the sound of bells, which were ringing in every village church, acted as the beacon for the passage of news.

Excitement rose as we neared the river and when we heard that Tony Venner's troop had run out of petrol some 10 miles short of the objective, our morale reached renewed heights. However, this was short lived, as although we managed a few more miles, Sgt Pritchard's tank spluttered and banged to a halt as we reached the main road at Quesnoy. We had travelled some 63 miles that day, 45 as the crow flies, and stopped two miles short of the bridge itself. The other troops of the squadron, who had been refuelled by the echelon earlier and had a few gallons of petrol into their tanks, reached the river. Unfortunately, when they got there they found that the bridge had been blown and despite searching north and south were unable to cross.

We halted in open country by the side of the road overlooking a small river. The wet weather had left us and it was a bright warm afternoon. We camouflaged ourselves as best we could under the circumstances, but did not feel any sense of threat, so I only had one man on guard on each tank, armed with a Sten gun in case any infantry appeared. There were few houses near us, but between us and the river there was a large barn. Bill Pritchard wandered off with his driver to have a look and a few minutes later reappeared with eight very frightened German soldiers. Apparently, he had opened the barn door and there were the soldiers lying down resting. They made no attempt to fight but stood up meekly leaving their weapons on the floor. They all lined up on the road looking pathetic, young, anxious, hollow-eyed and very apprehensive. None of us could speak much German, so any exchanges had to be by sign language. I was surprised at my feeling of friendliness towards them. I couldn't even dislike them and found myself wanting to offer them a meal while they waited to be collected.

My sentiments were not shared by all, and when I told one of the troop to collect their pay-books, he took the opportunity to go through their pockets, indicating that they should hand over their watches etc. When I saw this I was livid and made him return everything and leave them alone. It seemed totally wrong to me that because they were prisoners, we should rob them of personal items. Bill Pritchard disagreed with me, on the basis that as soon as they were back in the area of the prisoners' cages then others would take everything of value from them, the 'others' being people who had had no hand in their capture. While I could understand his argument I couldn't agree with it, and they left us with their personal possessions intact, we retaining their weapons. Perhaps I was wrong in adopting the attitude that I did, but then my father had been captured by Rommel in the desert, he had been well treated by the Germans which meant a lot to him, and I suppose that to some extent I reflected this.

During the late afternoon a wagon arrived from the echelon with petrol and supplies. As usual they had all the 'griff', and the rumour was that the division had run out of petrol, and we could be staying where we were for a few days while others, namely Patton and his Americans, went ahead. We were all starving by this time so we prepared a huge meal, banking on the fact that the rumour was true. Within minutes I was told to report to squadron HQ and returned from the 'O' Group with details of the next move which was immediate. We managed to finish our meal before moving. By 2100hrs we were back on the road in the gathering darkness. A bridge had been found just to the west of Amiens, and we were to cross that night. We joined the regiment just short of the bridge itself. It was more of a lock gate than a bridge and was near the village of Dreuil, a suburb of Amiens. We were all pretty tired by this time and were happy when we arrived at Vaux-en-Amiénois and went into harbour, it had been a long and exciting day.

Dawn on 1 September saw the regiment on the move again, although A Squadron were in reserve. We continued the advance at high speed in the direction of Doullens and St Pol, the latter being some thirty miles to our north. The battle for St Pol, which was a very tough one, was fought by B and C Squadrons, while we were used to support infantry, fill gaps in the line, or probe areas away from the main centre of the action. This very tiring process went on for two days until, on 2 September, we were instructed to join up with 22nd Armoured Brigade and lead the advance towards Ghent. We crossed the Arras–St Pol road and spent the night near Aubigny. We had hardly settled down in out blankets when we were told to stand to, as rumour had it that the Germans were attacking in force. Then B Squadron left the harbour to protect brigade HQ, and finally at about 0200hrs the whole regiment were alerted. We then formed a sort of 'box' in a large field, with three columns of tanks in lines of squadrons. Morning came with rain and cold winds and instead of the promised advance, we sat there waiting for orders. It was very galling, as the idea of being the 'liberators' of as large a city as Ghent appealed to us all. Eventually we were told that our petrol had been issued to other parts of the division and we were to remain in that area until supplies were available.

We were close to Béthune and Lens by this time, and the squadron reached the La Bassée Canal only to find that the bridge had been blown just as we arrived. It was a strange coincidence as far as I was concerned, as my father had served there during the First World War. The regiment was then instructed to find billets in houses around that area. We set up a squadron Officers' Mess in the Chateau des Prés, in Sailly-Labourse. This was a mining village on the outskirts of Béthune and although the populace were very poor, they were very welcoming and kind to us all. Madame Salmon, the wife of the owner of the Chateau, was most hospitable and gave up her sitting room and dining room without demur. I think that she enjoyed our visit in many ways, we certainly provided her with food supplies that she had not seen since the war started. She had a daughter of about 12 years old, who, in common with most of the children in the village, developed a great liking for army chocolate. This was the first time that we experienced cigarettes as the main-line currency, but they were accepted in all the local shops and bars in preference to our invasion money.

Close to the village was a mine shaft and, adjacent to it, a towering heap of spoil on top of which was the French flag. The mines had stopped working while the fighting was on, but rumour had it that the Maquis had thirty-five German prisoners down this shaft and were starving them to death. I was never able to determine the truth of the matter. This was an area populated by expatriate Polish miners; they were a very private section of the community and even their language was different. Their French accent was terribly hard to decipher. 'J'ie froo', they said, instead of 'J'ai froid', and when they spoke quickly among themselves, I had great difficulty in understanding a word they said. The cafés were full of happy people and, despite our impatience to move and rejoin the division, it was very pleasant to rest among such friendly folk.

One day an elderly couple came along the road and asked

to speak to a French-speaking officer. I was produced, and heard that they had a sister who lived in London and of whom they had had no word since 1940; did I perhaps know her? They then showed me the photograph of an elderly lady and her husband taken in Southend before the war. I explained that I lived in the country so I didn't actually know her, but did agree to send a letter through the army mail, provided that it was open and available to be censored. The next day they walked back again with a letter for their sister and gave me their card, which I have still. It is inscribed from Madame Kubis of Beuvry, and says 'Auriez la bonne volonté de mettre cette lettre dans votre courier. Je vous en remercie à l'avance. Reçevez mes sincères salutations.' I often wondered whether the lady had survived the bombing and whether they managed to renew their contact.

One of the funny experiences of the stay at Sailly-Labourse was to sleep in a real bed once more. I had thought that this would be utter bliss and could hardly wait to 'get my head down' on the first night. In fact I found the bed too soft and slept very badly, so the next night I used my camp bed, which was rarely used anyway. I slept much better. At the end of a week of enforced idleness, during which we were able to fully maintain our vehicles, clean out lockers, re-stow the ammunition and get our laundry done, we were all keen to move on. Alan Howard gave me a copy of a letter written to his brother Fred, which makes interesting reading and is a fair commentary on the times.

7 September 1944

Dear Fred

Don't think I am going soft using pink paper, but I think the ex-owner must have used it for writing to his fraulein – he won't need it now so I am using it up for him. I am very well and in pretty good spirits. We are at present still in France but quite close to the Belgium frontier. Where we go from here I don't know and I don't particularly care if we never move. We led the way here across the Seine and the Somme after those day and night drives you read about, and we were first into this place which is a mining town. The push here was tiring but very little opposition, but the welcome we received and are still receiving is terrific. You just had to stop for fear of running over people and, just like on films, we were showered with flowers, apples, pears, given wine, eggs, bread, in fact I think everything that they can possibly spare. At this moment, I am sitting in a miner's kitchen writing this letter and with my smattering of French, my little dictionary and plenty of patience on their part I get along OK. Every half hour or so a cup of coffee is produced and then the cognac, carefully hoarded for nearly five years for just this day.

The help given us since the break through by the FFI is really amazing. They are armed with all sorts of weapons, old French arms, captured or stolen German arms, hand grenades, bottles, anything in fact, and their enthusiasm and real hatred of the Germans amazes the unenthusiastic British soldier. In this small place alone, six FFI have been killed in the last few days rounding up stragglers, as they are doing most of this work for us, and the Jerries, especially the SS are dead scared to surrender to them, not without reason I think. Three SS were thrown off the top of one of the slag heaps here just before we arrived and they still have 30 SS and two collaborators down one of the shafts, 400 feet down and they have been there eight days, but what they have suffered seems to me to justify their attitude: seventeen women and children, eyes gouged out and hands cut off publicly for reprisal against the FFI and I myself saw the results of the massacre of a farmer and his family of seven for refusing food. The mentality of these maniacs is beyond my comprehension.

Yesterday was another celebration – 35 women became hairless for consorting with the German soldiers, one of them the wife of a French PoW with a little Boche around the house. It seems to me a rotten way to treat women but I suppose it's a different mental make-up from the French.

This is the third day we have been here now and there are still crowds around the tanks. It gets a bit monotonous but I suppose this is a great time for all of them, but you just can't move without a crowd of kids at your heels, screaming 'Cigarette for papa,' 'bully beef,' 'biscuit,' 'bon bon' and 'chocolate'. Papa has cost me about 300 fags from my stock and all my chocolate ration so far, it's got to the stage where you smoke a pipe in self defence – but it's still worth it to see people so happy again. All along the roads up here it was the same, cheering people and loads of flowers, and I discovered why the French always prefer wine – their beer is terrible.

The roads here are littered with battered Jerry kit, a tribute to the air force; the worst part was to see all the horses lying dead. The amount of horse transport they must have been compelled to use is amazing, showing that Bomber Command attacks on the oil industry has been worth it. Prisoners testify that they have to account for every litre and one told us that they have plenty of fighters in Germany but they have no petrol for them. Most prisoners seem to have reconciled themselves to the fact that they have lost the war, but blame their officers for deserting them, and the FFI stabbing them in the back, but some of the young ones still think they will win, on what other grounds than Goebbels they base their assumption, I don't know.

It was lovely weather until last night, then the weather broke and it is cold and now at 1.30pm it still hasn't stopped raining and outside is the legendary French mud. All over this area you see signs of the last war, old trenches and names with towns and dates cut in trees which have doubled their size since the letters were cut.

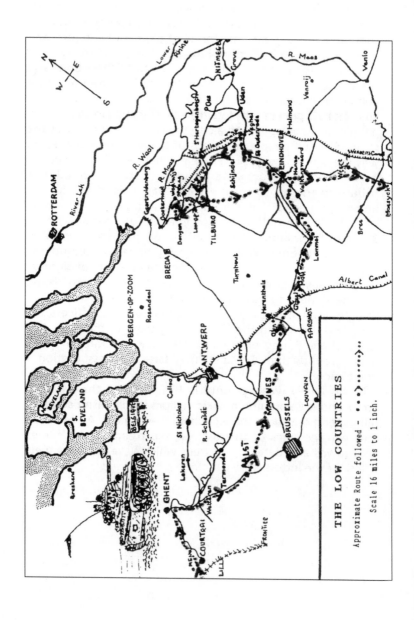

THE LOW COUNTRIES

Approximate Route followed – ●●>●●●●>●●

Scale 16 miles to 1 inch.

EIGHT

Holland and the Corridor

On the evening of 10 September, having been refuelled, we received orders to move up into Belgium, and we crossed the frontier on 11 September at a point between Menin and Courtral. The countryside of Belgium seemed ugly and flat after the lovely rolling pasture lands that we had seen on our way through France, the roads were straight, cobbled, and had a terrific camber which made tank driving very difficult as one tended to slide off to the side of the roads. The Belgian people received us with rapture and I shall never forget their noisy welcome. We were not the first British troops they had welcomed, but they all made us feel good. They handed out fruit and flowers to us, cheered and waved, and if we had to stop, rushed over to the tanks and tried to get on them and sit there waving to their friends and singing. We became ready targets for girls of all ages to kiss, but in common with most of the others, I soon found that as you were unable to be selective it was best to duck. We finished up in a harbour between Bavegem and Vlierzele, just outside Aalst, which is half way between Ghent and Brussels. A few of us went into the outskirts of Ghent that evening but there was still fighting going on in the area of the docks. Next day we went on to join the division at Malines and on 15 September were sent up to the famous Albert Canal. It all seemed to be very much a repeat of the First World War and my father would have been very much at home.

My troop was ordered to take up position on the canal bank overlooking a village, Grobbendonk, near the small town of Herenthals. We were to stop any enemy from crossing and to observe and report any movement. It all seemed very relaxed and, lulled into a false sense of security by our recent experiences, I was not as alert as usual. We drove in line ahead down the little road from Olen. There was a huge embankment along our side of the canal; this was about 40 feet high and completely blocked off the view. Instead of stopping, climbing the embankment and having a good look before proceeding, I decided to drive on to the point where the road turned north in order to inspect the bridge, which had been reported as blown. As we approached it, the road turned sharply to the right and passed through a deep cutting in the embankment. Before I had time to tell Chamberlain to stop, we were through the gap and poised, teetering on the edge of the wreckage of the blown bridge which ran down into the canal. Luckily I had halted the other two tanks of the troop, who by then were about 200 yards behind us and had had the good sense to stay under cover.

As I started to assess the situation, all hell was let loose and the tank juddered under the impact of shells striking the front glacis plate. I ducked instinctively into the turret and was unable to see where the firing was coming from, but reversed out as fast as possible while our machine-guns were fired at random. It was all over in a minute and as we had no HE shells up the spout at the ready, we didn't have time to fire the main armament. As soon as we had regained the protection of the embankment, and some of our composure, I left the tank under cover, and Alan Howard and I made our way, albeit cautiously, up the back of the bank to the top.

The view was fantastic and we could see Grobbendonk very clearly a couple of miles away and to our left. Below us was the canal and on the far bank about a mile away, driving at break-neck speed along the road, was a German truck on the back of which was mounted a 20mm multi-barrelled Oerlikon. What a fool I had been not to stand my ground and destroy it. However by now it was too late try to engage it, so we set up a look-out post at the top, eventually running a telephone down to my tank and we settled down to watch. Again it was a lovely soft warm day and we took it in turns to keep guard and man the lookout post. I was not going to be caught out again.

As soon as all this had been organised I went and inspected 'Abbot of Chantry'. We had received a lot of hits during our brief encounter and everyone told me that I would be astonished at the results. I certainly was. The shells had penetrated the armour plate to the extent of about two inches and had stuck in it, looking as if they had been spot welded on. I asked for Bill Best to come up from the LAD and have a look when he had time, and sure enough a short while later, up he came on his old motorbike. He was as nonplussed as we all were, and went back to check it out. The upshot of the matter was that, having checked the serial number, he found that I had been issued with an unarmoured training tank! Our beloved

'Abbess' was made from soft steel and was lighter than the others, which explained why she was so much faster, but wouldn't have stopped much except 20mm shells. I was offered a replacement tank, but we all wanted to keep her and despite a great deal of pressure from outside we managed to persuade them that for us she was a 'must'.

The position which we were occupying was absolutely fascinating as we could see a great deal of enemy movement, comprising infantry and soft vehicles. Occasionally we were able to direct the gunners as they carried out a shoot into the village itself, but for the most part it was the usual watching role. By plotting the comings and goings of the German vehicles we located the enemy headquarters, which was a café, and chased them out of that with some accurate shelling. During the afternoon it became apparent that they knew where we were, as they started shelling us in return, but none of it was close enough to cause us much worry. That evening a platoon of the Queens plus a gunner OP took over from us and we went back into harbour.

The regiment stayed in the area carrying out various roles of this nature and were still there on 19 September, when the endless lines of gliders flew over on their way to Arnhem and the airborne landings. I can remember it well, because at the time the troop was in a second line defence position and we had a grandstand view. It was a grey day and they looked so small and so vulnerable as they made their way slowly across the sky. The towing aircraft seemed to be fairly steady but many of the gliders were yawing up and down behind them. I was glad that we were fighting in established positions and on the ground. We didn't really know what was going on until somewhat later in the day, when we picked up the news on the radio from BBC London.

During the next two days, we gathered that despite the initial successes, all was not well either at Arnhem or along the corridor leading to it. The Guards Armoured Division and

1. The author during his school holidays in Torquay, Easter 1941. *(Author)*

2. No. 24 Troop, Sandhurst, early 1943. (*Author*)

3. Loading tanks on to trains at Brandon sidings, April 1944.
(Tank Museum, 880/B5)

4. A Squadron officers, June 1944. *(Author)*

5. Driving into 3 feet of water, 9 June 1944. *(Author)*

6/7. Relaxing in a troop leaguer, June 1944. *(Tank Museum 4546/D4 and 4547/A5)*

8. A flail tank of the 2nd County of London Yeomanry (Westminster Dragoons) in a Normandy village, June 1944. *(Author)*

9. Road into Villers-Bocage, June 1944. *(Author)*

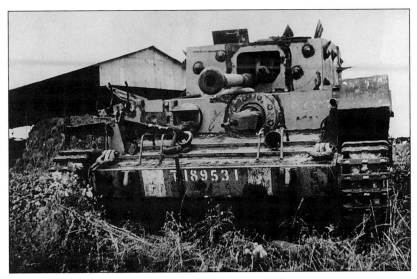

10. A Cromwell knocked out by 88-mm fire. *(Author)*

11. Little Audrey, Abbess of Chantry. *(Author)*

12. Operation Goodwood, 18 July 1944. *(IWM B7740)*

13. A Cromwell with searchlights fitted for the night advance on Caen, July 1944. *(Tank Museum 622.71)*

14. Armoured fighting vehicles of 7th Armoured Division assemble prior to Operation Goodwood, July 1944. *(Tank Museum 4811/B2)*

15. A Cromwell of the 2nd Northamptonshire Yeomanry, 11th Armoured Division. *(Author)*

16. Lisieux Basilica. *(Author)*

17. Recovering a Challenger tank. *(Author)*

18. The author's MC presentation by Field Marshal Montgomery. *(Author)*

19. Bill Bellamy, spring 1945. *(Author)*

20. Loading ammunition into a dug-in Cromwell tank, December 1944. *(Author)*

21. Temporary bridge over the Rhine, 23 March 1945. *(Author)*

22. Ruins of Xanten bridge. *(Author)*

23. Chaffee tank. *(Tank Museum 3014/C2)*

24. Passing PoWs in Hamburg. *(Author)*

25. Jack Ladenburg (adjutant 8th King's Royal Irish Hussars), Adam Hepburn and Douglas Rampf on a bridge over the Kiel Canal. *(Author)*

26. Monty with the Russian generals Zhukov, Rokossovsky, Malinin and Sokolovsky, to whom he presented medals on behalf of George VI, 12 July 1945. *(Author)*

27. The author's Chaffee in the Victory Parade, 21 July 1945. *(Author)*

28. Author after promotion to captain, August 1945. *(Author)*

29. Recce Troop, 8th King's Royal Irish Hussars, Berlin 1945. Captains Tim Pierson and Bill Bellamy are seen in the centre front. (Author)

others had fought with tremendous gallantry to achieve the impossible, but were now so thinly stretched that reinforcements were vital. The road was being cut and convoys of critical supplies could not get through. Units of the American 101 Airborne Division were holding bridges on the route up, but were not in direct contact with each other. In fact the situation was difficult, with the enemy on both sides of the corridor.

The regiment was moved east beyond Geel and then on 23 September came the news that we were to go north, pass through Eindhoven and deploy to keep the corridor to Nijmegen open. We were told that it was now threatened by strong German forces and was cut frequently. As seemed usual on these occasions, we had no sooner started to move than the heavens opened. We trundled our way through the bleak, flat, afforested heathlands near to Mol and Lommel, reaching Eindhoven in the late morning. If the drive had been miserable, the ensuing wait was worse. We harboured at Heeze, a village just inside Holland, the rain drenched us and we sat in silent dripping misery. Not a happy day. At the O Group that night we were given orders to pass through Eindhoven and, with the Queens, to clear the centre line between St Oedenrode and Veghel, 10–15 miles north of the city.

We moved out on 25 September, skirting the city itself to the west, but passing along the main road in front of the huge Philips factory, where a lot of the German war equipment was made and which had been extensively bombed. The squadron halted there for some time and a group of very wet but happy Dutch workers came along and presented me with a wireless set, filched from the factory. I used it for many years after the war, as it was a battery portable. We gave them some cigarettes and biscuits, which pleased them too. The roads were solid with lorries and, although we were a priority and they had pulled soft vehicles into the side of the road, it was very difficult to get the tanks through, as there were ambulances and other vehicles trying to come south at the same time. I have never seen quite such a scene, pouring rain, lorries of all shapes and sizes drawn up on the verges, dejected sodden drivers, irate military police trying to get the fighting troops through, and bunches of civilians waving and cheering despite the weather. The situation continued for some miles and then gradually we came into open country again and arrived at St Oedenrode. The road had just been opened, so our specific role had been superseded, and we were ordered to take up temporary positions around the town.

On the morning of 26 September we were sent out to the western side of the village, with orders to fence off the road towards Holland. It was another depressing day as we heard that the Arnhem garrison had had to be withdrawn, which seemed hard after all the efforts that had been made. However, the weather had improved and the country was more open, so we could see some distance over the fields and hedges. We advanced astride a minor road leading west out of the village, with my troop on the northern side of it. Although we didn't really expect much trouble, we had been told that there were a lot of enemy about, especially in the direction of Schijndel to our north-west.

I moved the troop forward slowly, trying to establish where the enemy positions lay, and after going for about two miles could see the railway track just to our north, but still had not made contact. We crossed a small bridge over a drainage dyke, fanned out again, broke through a hedge almost in line and found ourselves in the middle of the German positions. They must have heard our approach, but rather late, as of the group of four 88mm guns which were in the centre of the adjacent field, two were still in an anti-aircraft attitude, pointing to the sky, but the other two had traversed on to us. Instinctively we all fired our 75mm guns and machine guns. I fired the smoke canisters on the side of the turret and ordered everyone back through the hedge at maximum speed. The odds were too great, there were Germans everywhere, and as we shot through the hedge we were accompanied by 88mm shells, small arms and, I imagine, anything else that they could find to throw at us.

This rousing reception lent us wings and we flew across the next field, realising too late that the drainage dyke was blocking our path and the only bridge was not for some 300 yards to our left, but also in the adjacent field. There was nothing for it but to act like steeple-chasers and jump it. I had done this sort of thing at Bovington when I was involved in a series of tank trials in early 1942, but the idea of doing it in the heat of the moment had not entered into my head. The only thing that I did remember was to shout, 'Dip your clutch,' to Chamberlain, who probably knew anyway. Luckily the dyke on our side had a slight ramp up to the edge and we hit this at a good 20mph. Our tank rose in the air and landed on the other bank with a great crunch. Things flew about in the turret, Smith was badly bruised as the remaining shells, which he still had on his knee, hit him in the face and shoulder, and we were all shaken. Our lot was as nothing to Bill Pritchard and Alan Howard; they were some 100 yards behind us and seeing our success, emulated our example. Bill Pritchard's tank hit it well and landed as we had, except that his driver forgot to de-clutch. The tank almost came to a halt with a scream of protesting gears, it pitched up on to its nose and the bedding rolls and other items stowed on the back flew in a great parabola over the top of the tank into the field.

Meanwhile Alan Howard, whose tank was slower, had taken off, but his bedding rolls were dropping like bait into the water. He just made the far edge of the dyke, teetered there and then by some miracle the tracks bit and he pulled up the bank. We drove on across the next field and then reformed in the hedge where we remained while shelling and mortaring continued in our general area. We were very lucky not to have had a track break on landing and I felt that our guardian angel had really pulled out all the stops this time! Some days later, when the area had been cleared we went back to the dyke and measured the width of it; it was about 20 feet at the point where we had jumped!

The general level of activity increased as the day went on and the shelling became very bad. We were not far from Tony Venner's troop and they suffered more accurate attention than us, Tony being killed by shellfire later that day. He was a great loss, and, like Tim Pierson and Frank Saxby, was one of the officers who had joined us from the 2nd Northamptonshire Yeomanry on 28 August after they had been disbanded. Tony Hind and I were now the only two original troop leaders in the squadron to have survived from Normandy.

We stayed in the general area of St Oedenrode for some days, the weather remained settled, and as the pressure began to ease, we were given time to go back to Eindhoven, have hot baths, visit a sort of Officers' Club in a hotel south of the city and even go to the cinema. We became very friendly with the troops of the 101 Airborne Division (USA), who had captured St Oedenrode bridge at the time of the Arnhem landings. They were avid collectors of Luger pistols, one of which I had been lucky enough to pick up during the fighting near Mont Pinçon. I was able to exchange this for an American repeating rifle, with a couple of boxes of ammunition. When I enquired as to whether its owner would miss it, I was told laconically that, 'Where he was, he wouldn't be needing a rifle any more.' It was an invaluable weapon, accurate, and holding 13 rounds. I used it militarily on a number of occasions, but certainly the most famous one occurred while another young officer and I, out shooting hares, were unaware that Colonel Cuthie and the brigadier were shooting on the other side of a bank in the same field. We started a hare which ran left-handed; we followed it with repeated shots from our rifles, missed it, but put both of our senior officers deep into a drainage dyke. They were not very pleased and we received the most imperial rollicking. I also obtained a splendid fur-collared windproof flying jacket which I wore throughout the ensuing winter.

We were usually sited in positions which covered one of the tracks leading into St Oedenrode and, once the tanks were settled in, we used to have a competition to see who could create the best camouflage. We had done this one day and were sitting on top of my tank, talking quietly and keeping watch, when two parachutists from 101 Airborne wandered down the track towards us as if they were out on a Sunday school picnic. They stopped literally within three feet of the front of my tank and stood there talking, while they took out their cigarettes. Allen, who was not lacking in humour, tossed a box of matches down to them, which landed at their feet and one of them bent down to pick it up thinking that the other had dropped it. Suddenly they both realised that this had come from some other agency and they looked around them with some agitation. They still didn't spot the tank but I felt that we could have an accident if we didn't declare ourselves, so I stood up and said, 'OK, relax, we're British,' and climbed down the front of the tank to join them. They were quite stunned to find that they were standing within a few feet of a British tank and clearly quite impressed. They came back later with a load of rations which varied the menu a bit, although I never really liked Vienna sausages.

At the end of the month we left St Oedenrode and went up to Veghel, which was only a few miles to the north, over the Willems Vaart Canal. The winter began to clamp down, and activity, on our front at least, was minimal. I went down to Brussels for the first time from here, and spent two nights with Bob Ames and Tony Hind in a hotel on the Boulevard Adolphe Max reserved for officers on leave. I was very unsophisticated and didn't really taste the delights of that great city. In the end, they rather left me to it and I went to the Officers' Club in the Rue de la Loi, drank too much and was brought back to the hotel with a bunch of other young friends in a not dissimilar condition. I purchased a few lace handkerchiefs and a couple of prints, went to the cinema, and was really quite happy when the time came to return to the regiment. Others had lurid tales of their amatory exploits to recount, but I was unable to match them. I realised that I had wasted an opportunity to enjoy myself, it was no use moping about Audrey and not letting my hair down when the chance arose, and I determined to enjoy the next visit.

This was one of the many periods in my life when I wrestled between the moral values that had been instilled in me by the Dominicans and the attractions of the pleasures which surrounded me. Life was hazardous and on occasion it seemed to me that if I didn't grasp the opportunities presented to me, then I could die without having 'lived', whatever that meant. Equally, I had been brought up to believe in fidelity and had a great respect for and love of women. I had not been sexually awakened and although curious, and sometimes envious of graphic, and now I realise, wildly exaggerated accounts of other fellow exploits; I didn't really find it too difficult to remain as an onlooker. I was a romantic at heart and I didn't want to find that love could be soiled in any way. I see from my note books, that during this period, I started to write prose and poetry again. This was a sure sign of the inner conflict which I was experiencing.

I am sure that in different ways most of us were going through the same adolescent pains. Despite this I had a marvellous time with the other young officers in the regiment.

There was a great deal of horse-play, there were the in-jokes particular to our little society, and there were bouts of happy drinking which left us with headaches but no other serious effects. I enjoyed my life to the full within my self-imposed limitations. I don't think that they considered me to be a prig, and if they did then it was well concealed. I was naive, unsophisticated and inexperienced, I was known to be strongly Catholic in my views and that in turn led to some fairly solid but good-natured leg pulling.

The activity at this time was constant but not very demanding. We were facing the German 'Stomach' Division, which we were told, was composed of low medical category soldiers who needed milk and special diet in order to carry out their duties. Despite their handicaps they fought extremely well. Perhaps their dyspepsia helped them to hate us. We evolved a routine, almost as if we were going to the office. There was an 'O' Group at night, discussion of the days events, allocation of positions to be occupied the next day, leave at dawn or thereabouts, day out on standing patrol and home at last light. The enemy were not very aggressive, in fact the most aggressive person in the area was the heavily decorated commanding officer of the 1/5th Queens. He ran a series of the most bloodthirsty exercises in the deserted village of Dinther. These were designed to train his men and us, in the 'not so gentle art' of house-to-house fighting. I have a feeling that he was Welsh in origin. The whole exercise was done at the double, and his shouts of, 'Grenades through downstairs window – fire Sten through door – door down – grenade top of stairs – rooms to right and left – fire Sten through the ceilings – up the stairs – grenades through doors – etc,' still ring in my ears. He was a tonic, and we blessed his foresight during the fighting which lay ahead.

It was obvious to us all that the time was fast approaching when there would be a battle to clear the Germans out of south-west Holland and free the port of

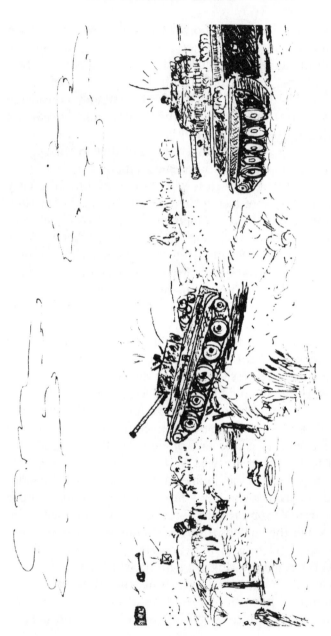

----THERE WAS NOTHING FOR IT BUT TO ACT LIKE STEEPLECHASERS AND JUMP IT!

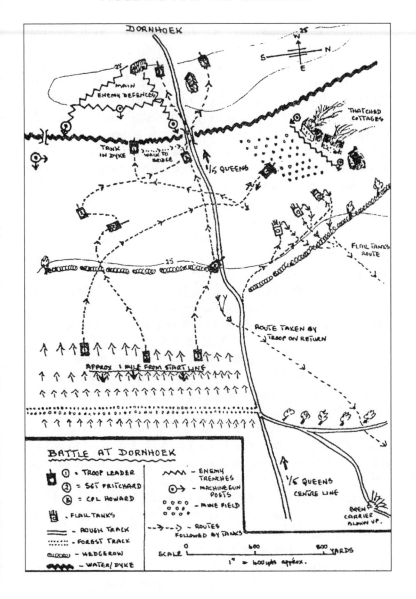

DORNHOEK

MAIN ENEMY DEFENCES

THATCHED COTTAGES

TANK IN DYKE
WALK TO BRIDGE

1/5 QUEENS

FLAIL TANKS ROUTE

15

ROUTE TAKEN BY TROOP ON RETURN

APPROX 1 MILE FROM START LINE

1/5 QUEENS CENTRE LINE

BREN CARRIER BLOWN UP.

BATTLE AT DORNHOEK

① = TROOP LEADER
② = SGT PRITCHARD
Ⓗ = CPL HOWARD

🚩 = FLAIL TANKS

— = ROUGH TRACK
...... = FOREST TRACK
((((((((= HEDGEROW
〰〰〰 = WATER/DYKE

ᗯᗯ — ENEMY TRENCHES
⊙→ — MACHINE GUN POSTS
▫▫▫ — MINE FIELD
– →–→ – ROUTES FOLLOWED BY TANKS

SCALE
0   600   800   YARDS
1" = 600 yds approx.

139

Antwerp from any further threat. The weather was deteriorating, it was wet and very cold and the snow of winter was in the offing. News of the next major operation, code named 'Alan', was given out on 21 October. The division was to advance towards the town of 's-Hertogenbosch and we were to take part in the opening breakout, assisted by the 1/5th Queens. A Squadron was to advance with three troops up, Frank Saxby on the right, Tony Hind in the centre and my troop on the left. Our objective was to clear the small hamlet of Doornhoek. The countryside was comprised of heathland, with pinetree woods divided up by sandy tracks where mines could be laid easily and remain unseen. There were arable areas, but poor, with small boggy fields surrounded by drainage dykes. The going in these areas was wet and treacherous.

I thought long and hard about this battle. We were to lead off ahead of the infantry, we knew that the enemy were well dug-in and had had more than enough time to complete their defences, and that there could be no element of surprise. I expected to encounter minefields and scatter mines all over the approaches. When I held troop orders that evening, I surprised them all by reversing our usual strategy. I had decided that we would advance one tank up rather than the usual two, and I stressed that 'under no circumstances' would any tank, at any time, drive along a track. I wanted to reduce the actual troop committal to the minimum until we saw what we were up against. That evening we had a good hot supper, all together under one bivvy and I for one, slept like a log. The troop were very good about things like guard duties when we were actually involved in battles, I was excluded from the roster, which means that I had an unbroken night's sleep. I certainly appreciated it.

The morning of 22 October was grey, damp and foggy; visibility was such that we couldn't actually begin the advance until about 0700hrs. Tony, Frank and I huddled together in the lee of Tony's tank talking, laughing and smoking endless cigarettes until the order to move came. It is a day etched in my mind from beginning to end. At the Start Line, I decided to change the pattern of the troop advance as the country was more heath-like than I had envisaged. Accordingly, we advanced in line for the first half a mile or so. Frank was suffering from verbal diarrhoea and totally monopolised the squadron wireless net. Tony, I heard later, was as infuriated as I was by this, as neither of us could report our progress. After about half an hour, we came to the end of the heather and into a wide belt of pine trees. There was a broad ride to our right and a somewhat thinner belt of trees to our left. I ignored the ride and took the troop through the trees but in a triangular formation with my tank leading. As we wove our way through the trees, there was a violent explosion to our right-hand and in one of the moments when Frank was quiet, I heard Tony's troop sergeant report that Tony's tank had just gone up on a mine. A few minutes after this Tony himself came on the air to say that his driver was badly wounded – he survived to return to the regiment – and that the mine had broken his track and blown off the front idler wheel. It was a relief to know that the damage had not been worse. I was ordered to cover to my right and try to fill the gap.

We reached the end of the woodland belt and stopped in a hedge abutting a number of small grassy fields. These led down to a wide dyke about 400 yards away, which ran across our front from left to right. Behind the dyke, but very indistinct in the mist which still clouded our view, was what looked like the enemy redoubt, sited adjacent to the track which ran diagonally from our right rear and crossed the dyke by a small wooden bridge. About 150 yards to the right of this track and at right angles to it there lay a group of thatched cottages. The track was Tony's original centre-line and it was clear that I must now move to my right and test out the defences there as the infantry needed to cross that bridge if they were to advance.

Leaving the other two tanks in the edge of the woodland to give me cover, I advanced diagonally to the right towards the track. I had my turret lid open but otherwise we were totally closed down, and Chamberlain was driving using only his periscopes. There was a continual flurry of small arms fire and some mortar bombs coming from the main German company position to my left, but so far nothing to suggest anti-tank guns. We halted just over the track and eventually located the machine-guns that were causing the problem. They, coupled with snipers, were in the three thatched houses now some 100 yards to my front. The shots were uncomfortably close, pinging off the armour plate. At that moment, three flail tanks of the Westminster Dragoons appeared through the hedge about 300 yards to my right. They advanced majestically towards the cottages, their chains flailing the ground ahead, so as to explode any mines which may have been there. The three tank commanders were standing up in their turrets directing the operation, apparently totally unaware that there was so much small arms fire in their vicinity. I suppose that the noise of the flails deadens all other sounds. Before I could wave or drive over or even find out their wireless frequency, two of the tank commanders were shot dead and all three tanks turned and disappeared back into the woods.

It was our general policy to try to avoid destroying houses unless vital to the success of an operation. We were all very conscious that the winter was near and that the Dutch still had to live somewhere when we had gone. The three cottages however, housed aggressive troops who were holding up our advance and they had to be neutralised. I was just about to call forward Corporal Howard and attack them from the left and right when a well placed burst of Schmeiser fire hit the joint of my turret flaps, spraying my face with minute particles of molten lead! This latter had happened to me on a previous occasion and left blue dots such as our village smith at Cranford used to have on his face and hands before the war. They disappeared in a couple of days. Although it didn't actually hurt, it really annoyed me and I called for the other two tanks to ease forward until they had a good field of fire. Then, without further delay, we set about brewing up the houses and clearing the Germans out.

The straw roofs caught fire very satisfactorily and while the troop fired shells and machine-gunned the area, I edged forward gradually until I was about 50 yards from the centre house. Suddenly a number of Germans ran out of the houses and jumped into a trench in front of the left-hand house. Allen gave them a couple of personal HE rounds with our 75mm gun, and seconds later the butt of a rifle appeared above the trench waving in the air with a whitish handkerchief tied to it. I shouted 'Come out' to them but all they did was carry on waving. At that moment Allen asked Smithie to load an armour piecing shot and he then fired directly at the rifle butt. That brought them out! I then signalled to them to run across to us, but one of them pointed at the ground on which we stood and shouted, 'Minen, Minen'! (minefield) and with their hands up they ran along the front of the house to our right and towards our lines, where I presume that they were picked up by the infantry.

The burning thatches made a great deal of smoke and this, coupled with the mist, made visibility very difficult. I resolved therefore that if, as appeared likely, my tank was either in or on the edge of a minefield, I would reverse it out covered by the other two tanks and then move in my tank towards the bridge. Meanwhile as the mist cleared a little, the small arms fire had increased from the area of the main redoubt. This lay about 400 yards to my left, and I delayed my move while the other two tanks re-sited themselves in order to give me some cover. They had just got into position when Bill Pritchard came on the B set shouting, 'Your tank is on fire!' I looked back over the engine covers and saw all our bedding blazing, the spare battery was on its side and one of the two jerrycans which I had carried on the mudguards, illegally, since we ran out of petrol in France, had fallen over and was spewing out petrol. Luckily this was running over the side and not on to the red hot exhaust pipe, which was about three feet away from it. I must confess to a complete sense of panic for a moment. There was still a great deal of small arms fire rattling around, and for us to try and evacuate the tank would have been suicide. We couldn't let it go on burning because the petrol would ignite and the end result would be equally disastrous. We were probably in a minefield so I couldn't go forward and get behind the buildings. My best option, perhaps my only one, was to reverse out on the same tracks which I used coming in, as that was the only route which I knew to be clear. However, the fire was increasing in intensity and if I reversed, then the flames and smoke would fill the turret, choking the crew. I knew that the only answer was to get out and cut off the bedding rolls and ditch the jerrycan, but I felt very frightened at the thought of having to leave the shelter of the tank.

I grabbed one of our phosphorous smoke grenades from the rack, and in my nervousness, unwound the release tape and pulled out the safety pin, which prevents it from igniting. Luckily I was still holding on to the handle of the release mechanism itself. Then quite suddenly, I realised what a fool I was being and felt absolutely calm, almost as if I was detached from it all. I threw the smoke grenade over the left-hand side of the tank and jumped out on to the engine covers. It took a matter of seconds to remove the jerrycan of petrol and hurl that as far as I could over one side, before cutting off the bedding rolls and chucking them over the other.

The battery was stowed on the right-hand side, on the mudguard and just behind the turret. I couldn't get at it easily so I jumped down on to the ground. I remember picking up my beret which was lying on the ground and putting that back on my head. As I did so I happened to look down and was horrified to see that the right-hand track of our tank was actually resting on the edge of a Teller mine. These, as the name suggests, were mines made up of two plates. The outer one which was about 18 inches wide formed the canister holding the explosive and the smaller, inner one, more like a saucer in size, stood on top of it and formed the pressure pad, which, when touched, caused the mine to explode. We had escaped from being blown up by about an inch. The central plate, the pressure pad, was actually touching the edge of the track and the mine itself was tipped up at an angle of about 45 degrees. I hesitated as to whether I should try and slide the mine out from under the track, but decided that it was too firmly wedged. At that moment there was a further flurry of small arms fire striking the other side of the tank and I felt that the mortaring could start any minute. Keeping under the lee of the hill, I righted the battery, clambered back into the turret and told Chamberlain that under no circumstances was he to touch his steering, but he was to reverse out very slowly. This we did without further worry and having regained the other side of the track, we turned, headed towards the centre of the enemy redoubt and started to advance again.

As soon as we moved, a Spandau (machine-gun) sited to our left front sprayed the tank from close quarters. All three of the tanks fired back and this flushed a couple of Germans into

the open. Bill Pritchard, who was commanding the left-hand tank, dealt with them and we continued our slow progress, firing as we went, with the intention of stopping at the edge of the dyke. We were advancing parallel to the track about 200 yards to the left of the bridge and I was concentrating all my attention on the redoubt. Suddenly the mist lifted momentarily, and for the first time I saw clearly in front of us the whole line of German trenches. They were full of panic-stricken men running in all directions and as they were only about 60 yards from me I could see them in great detail. The roofs of the trenches themselves were partially covered with wood which had sods of earth on top. The main trench ran parallel to the dyke; at either end there was a short stub trench leading to a machine-gun post, from each of which there were men running back towards the main defences. In the centre of the foremost trench stood two German officers in their greatcoats, neither appearing to move, nor to be taking part in the proceedings. It was an extraordinary sight and both of my gunners opened up with their machine-guns before I had even given them an order to do so.

I had intended to call for the other two tanks to come up but they were already firing as hard as they could and further moves were unnecessary. In the meantime Chamberlain, who was still driving in the closed up position and only able to use his periscope, was slowly inching our tank forward. In the excitement of the moment I failed to realise that he hadn't seen the dyke. The next minute we plunged down the sloping side of it into about three feet of water. The turret was completely open to the Germans, who luckily didn't seem to be very interested, and when we tried to back out, the tank began to slew round and was in danger of tipping over. It was evident that there was no way that we could get out without a tow.

Seeing my predicament, the other two tanks closed up towards us to give us protection and Bill Pritchard reported that a company of the Queens, running along the track behind us and to our right, were now approaching the bridge. I told him to keep firing into the redoubt until they saw the infantry well across the bridge. I then called for Alan Howard to bring his tank forward to the side of the track by the bridge itself, so that I could take it over temporarily, and then asked him to transfer to my tank until it could be recovered. Bill Pritchard was to give me protective fire while I got out and made my way on foot along the back of the dyke to the bridge.

The mist came and went, shells and mortar fire fell near to the tank but then stopped. Chamberlain and Goldsworthy told me that they were both sitting up to their arses in freezing cold water and I replied that it was their fault. I instructed Allen and Smith to close the lid of the turret the moment that I was out and to keep it closed until they were told over the air to open it again and admit Alan Howard. No one was to get out. It was a beastly position for them to be in, as they could see absolutely nothing except the water and must have felt horribly vulnerable. I didn't want to get out of the tank and leave them, but I knew that I needed to be there when the infantry company commander came, so as to inform him of the situation.

When Alan Howard, whom I was unable to see, reported that his tank was in position, I opened the hatch, scrambled out of the tank, feeling that this was becoming rather a habit, and made my way along the bank towards the bridge. There was still quite a lot of firing, although mainly from small arms. When I was only a few yards from the bridge itself a burst of fire killed one member of the platoon of

our infantry who were running across it. I reached the bridge just as the company commander arrived in his Brengun carrier. He slowed down slightly, looked at me and before I could speak said, 'What the bloody hell are you doing here?' I was about to reply 'Waiting here for you for the last three hours!' but he did not wait for my reply, drove straight over the bridge and disappeared into the mist! I felt thoroughly deflated.

Bill Pritchard and I then took our two tanks across the bridge, deciding that it was not mined as the Brengun carrier had crossed it without trouble, and continued to provide forward cover. The main fighting in our immediate area now seemed to be over, the mist cleared, the sun came out and I became aware that it was now past 12 o'clock, that I was very hungry and desperately tired.

The objectives had been taken and secured with little loss of life and with a good haul of prisoners; we were ordered to move over to the right flank of the advance and take up a watching position some half a mile to our right rear. Apparently the 5th Royal Tanks were put in a set piece attack and we were to act as flank guard. I plotted the route on the map and off we went. I still insisted that we keep off the tracks as most of them had not yet been cleared and we made our way through the thin hedges taking a circuitous route. At one point we spotted squadron HQ away to our right and travelling towards them, from the direction of enemy lines, a Bren gun carrier of the Queens travelling at speed. It was on the main track and about 200 yards short of Squadron HQ, when there was the most almighty explosion, and we actually saw men and pieces of men hurled into the air. There must have been a 250lb bomb under the track as the carrier totally disintegrated. This was the sort of thing that I had foreseen at the 'O' Group on the previous evening, and I felt vindicated in my decision to stay off the tracks, a decision which, so they told me later, was applauded by the rest of the troop. We didn't stop at squadron HQ but went on to the rendezvous with the 5th Royal Tanks, made contact, and then settled down into our watching role. I was totally drained and, without waiting for food, lay down in the sunshine on a grassy bank and went straight to sleep.

I awoke refreshed a couple of hours later and found that 'Nell' Gwynne, our squadron leader, had visited us to congratulate the troop on its success during the morning battle, but had told Bill Pritchard to allow me to sleep on. By my side was an exciting looking package wrapped in a blanket and an expectant troop were sitting around waiting for me to open it. It was as if it was my birthday, as at the same time a huge plateful of hot fresh chicken stew appeared. I was urged to open the package first, and in it I discovered the most attractive linen tablecloth, beautifully hand- embroidered with flowers and motifs. Inside that was a wad of notes in 5 and 10 guilder denominations. I was a little apprehensive that while I slept some looting had taken place, but as soon as I finished my meal I was taken a few yards down the track and shown what was evidently a German loot wagon, piled high with household goods, chairs, a table, linen, blankets and bottled food stuff. Incidentally I still have the tablecloth at home and use it frequently. It has never ceased to give pleasure. The money I thought to be valueless and said so, as we had our own invasion currency. Later we were told that small denominational notes were still valid. My name was mud as we had used some as extra loo paper.

Later that evening I discovered that a bullet had actually passed through the flap of my beret leaving two holes. I had been very lucky. The bottled foodstuff was marvellous while it lasted and we enjoyed the change of diet. Beautiful chicken in jelly, runner beans, red and blackcurrants and a variety of other vegetables. Our troop mess became a popular rendezvous for the rest of the squadron.

Sometime earlier I had written an article entitled 'Troop Leaders for Orders' which, after much persuasion by the other troop leaders, I had submitted to *Men Only*. I received a letter from the editor thanking me for my literary effort, but declining to print it. I can understand why. It reads as follows:

Deep consoling sleep is broken. 'Wake up. Wake up.' Creeps realisation of the cold and the blackness. Furtive movements, whispered words, dry mouths formulate assent and hear, hollow through blanketed distance, 'Troop leaders for orders, sir.' Covers thrown aside and blindly searching for boots, map board and hat, the queasy stomach of early morning turns to the hollow pitted emptiness of pent up feeling and anticipation. 'Surely my troop is in reserve. O God it must be. Make it an easy job. I wonder where we are going to now?' These thoughts course feverishly through the mind while damp clothes cover a flinching body and the pulse beats abnormally quickly until there is no further excuse for lingering. Boots swish among the tall wet grass and saturated trousers flap against the legs. 'There he is. Thank God the others are there too. Am I late? No.' Sleepiness returns once more as maps are set and then the battle is drawn on them in different coloured chinagraphs. 'I would have that job! Why couldn't I do that troop's? I always lead.' Conflicting and distracting thoughts race through the brain and then suddenly – 'Any questions?' – and relief that despite the uncivil hour you had grasped it all. The long walk back, the troop conference. A sleepy somewhat outraged group of men packing the tanks and brewing the tea while the tank commanders cluster round to be put in the picture. Immediately all is well, you are awake and it is they who are sleepy. Orders are concise, positions are explained, a cup of tea, the roar of engines warming up, the crackling of the wireless and then the order to advance is given. In that first move, the brain is emptied of all distractions, the whole plan clears, the map stands out as a country with elevations, breadth and depth, the stomach settles, warms, retracts and normality returns, ousting fears and uncertainties.

I do not recall whether this portrays exactly how we felt but it was written at the time, and although probably rather romanticised, it contains a great deal of truth.

The next two days were spent in movements around the area of Doornhoek and Middlerode, but on 24 October we went to Schijndel. At the evening 'O' Group we were told the next day we would cross the river Dommel and continue our advance in the general direction of Oosterhout. It seemed a peculiar direction for an advance as we had turned our backs on the ultimate target which was of course Germany, and were attacking towards the west with the object of clearing the Germans out of the area south of the river Maas. In the event, the bridge which was necessary to our advances was not cleared, and late in the day we crossed the river at Esch and arrived in Udenhout which had been captured by the 1st Royal Tanks after a fierce struggle. Houses were blazing everywhere and it was obvious that the German infantry had needed to be driven out of each farm and building. We leaguered for the night near a gutted farmhouse and were pleased to be able to offer some hot food and drinks to a family sheltering there. Despite their plight, we gathered that they were happy to be free once more and to be rid of 'Der Moffe'. This was the time when the phrase, 'Alles Kaput, der Kinder sind in Keller, der Moffe aweg,' was heard. Loosely interpreted that meant, 'Everything has been destroyed, the children are safe in the cellar and the bloody Germans have gone!' We spent an uncomfortable night, and then were on call for the next day while the plan to clear the remainder of the area was prepared.

Late on the evening of 27 October we received orders to join the attack on Loon-op-Zand, and married up with the 1/7th Queens with the objective of mounting a preliminary attack that evening. C Squadron were already fighting out to the west of the village, but we remained concealed behind a small hill about 2 miles short of it. At about 1700hrs, in failing light as it was a very dull day, my troop was ordered to move on to Loon-op-Zand and, with Frank Saxby's troop on our right, we loaded up a couple of platoons of the Queens and advanced over the crest of the hill, some 400 yards to the east of the main Tilburg–Loon-op-Zand road.

As we reached the brow of the hill I noted that there was a small wood in front of us and I signalled to Frank that I would take the left-hand or road side of this, while he searched the other edge. We dismounted our infantry who ran on down the edge of the wood, and then we started off again towards the village. There was a very wide track in front of me and I took the left-hand side of this while Bill Pritchard stayed on the right, slightly behind me, followed directly by Alan Howard. The idea was that I would watch the road, which was only just discernible in the bad light, while they kept an eye on the infantry. We all had HE shells loaded in our 75mm guns.

Below us and about 1,000 yards away was the village, screened by trees, and just short of these, to my left front near a slight jink in the road, was a patch of bushes. There was something about them which worried me and I called to Allen to traverse on to them and tell me if he saw anything suspicious. After a few seconds he said he thought he might have seen movement and as it was such an obvious place for an anti-tank gun I told him to fire. It is difficult to separate the next series of events one from another. As Allen fired, so there was a brilliant flash from the bushes and simultaneously an incredible roar and a whooshing noise which seemed to envelop us. People always describe AP (armour-piercing) shots as sounding like an approaching express train and this to some extent described the noise that we heard at that moment. The shot, because that was what it turned out to be, came from a German 75mm anti-tank gun. It went diagonally from left to right, across the front of my glacis plate, missing us by inches, then struck the ground at the front of Bill Pritchard's tank, passed straight under it, emerged at the rear and ricocheted over Alan Howard's turret before disappearing noisily into the rear areas. Smith had loaded a second shell and that too Allen fired into the bushes to be rewarded by another flash but this time orange, which usually denoted a hit.

We continued to plaster the area with shots, but there was no further reply. Meanwhile the Queens, having reached the front edge of the wood, were ordered to call off the attack, as by now the light was too bad for us to give any support. They clambered aboard, we lifted them back to their night positions and rejoined the squadron, following the other troops into a leaguer around a large farm which had not been damaged in the fighting. I went over to talk to John Gwynne, who was busy reversing his tank up against the wall of the farmhouse. He was an officer to whom tanks were an incompre-hensible adversary. His only love was the horse and somehow tanks never did precisely what he intended. This did not make him a bad squadron leader, but did allow us to pull his leg unmercifully about matters technical. On this occasion he was standing in front of his tank guiding the driver as he reversed and using the normal control signals which had been evolved. Hold up right fist to brake left track, thus turning the tank's rear to its left, left fist right track, and hands waved across each other to signify stop and switch off. He achieved success with the angle at which he backed the tank up against the farm wall, but unfortunately he omitted to instruct the driver to stop. There was a dreadful crunch, and before I could stop it his tank had entered the farm kitchen and brought down a great chunk of wall which lay in a heap across its engine covers. The startled farmer with his wife and family came tumbling out to view the devastation. They were remarkably good about it, but it took a lot of time and ingenuity to bolster up the side of the building, extract John's tank and hang temporary tarpaulin covers over the gaping void. Enigmatic John seemed totally unmoved by the whole event.

Next morning we prepared to advance at first light, but were delayed by very heavy and accurate shelling which made life especially difficult for the infantry. Frank's and my troops were given the same roles as for the previous night and as left-hand troop, I decided to smoke off the small copse at the entrance to the village and then charge down it. We reached it to find, to Allen's satisfaction, that the 75mm gun had been totally destroyed and there were a number of dead Germans around it. Alan Howard took over the lead and we advanced, followed by the infantry, along the sides of the road through the avenue of tall trees. We had been ordered not to enter the town, so as we reached the first house, which was on the left side about 300 yards short of the crossroads in the town centre, we halted. There was a lot of firing, mainly from machine-guns, but the mortar fire was intense and, as much of it was bursting in the treetops, it made life very difficult for us. I noted that there was a long ditch running away to the right of the road and in front of it a patch of grass and leaves. I left Alan Howard as point tank on the left-hand side of the road, Bill Pritchard drew up to him on the right, and I went further over to the right on the grass. In this way we were enabled to bring three tanks' fire to bear on the houses and the crossroads ahead.

Meanwhile the infantry arrived and filed into the ditch slightly to my rear and were able to report that we had captured the 'castle', which was our initial objective. We were then told to await the arrival of a fresh company of the Queens and assist them forward into the village. I ordered the tanks to switch off and maintain quiet so that we could listen for any enemy movement, especially armour. C Squadron had reported that there were tanks or self-propelled guns moving about on the lateral road which bisected the village.

The mortaring was still heavy at this stage, but I had reached the end of my tether on a more pressing personal matter. I was a creature of regular habits and it was a long time past my normal hour. There was nothing for it but to jump out of the tank and before the delighted eyes of a company of the Queens to undress and allow nature to take its course. I received a great deal of good-humoured advice, with realistic grunts and groans. I had no sooner returned to my tank than a German self-propelled gun, with infantry running alongside it, crossed the crossroads ahead at speed. There were perhaps three seconds in which to fire and Bill Pritchard's gunner, Tpr Wills, blew the front idler wheel straight off it with a magnificent shot. It slewed into the cemetery on the opposite side of the road where it brewed up while we all fired our machine guns into the infantry running alongside it. I was linked direct to regimental HQ at the time, as they were controlling the arrival of the next infantry company, and was able to report that 'An enemy SP and infantry attacked from the cemetery area in Loon-op-Zand. They have all been knocked out and remain there.' Tony Case, the new adjutant, appreciated that.

The new company of the Queens arrived and after a brief consultation we started up again and began to bombard the houses to the left and right of the road leading to the crossroads. They then sent a platoon into the houses on either side of the road, and we arranged for a signal from the windows so that we could phase our firing to coincide with their advance. Just before they started I was standing talking to one of their sergeants, who turned to me and said, 'You see that corner building on the left there, sir? That's the bank. Break it open well for us!' I vowed to do just that.

Initially there was a lot of opposition and, despite shells at short range and the machine-gunning of the upper windows, the enemy managed to keep a constant stream of Schmeisser fire coming in our general direction. Alan

Howard, who was advancing up the left-hand side of the road, had a particularly difficult time with the close range grenades and Panzerfausts exploding around him. Then suddenly, almost dramatically, their firing became sporadic, the Queens burst out of the buildings just short of the crossroads and we saw them reach the corner buildings on either side. These included the bank. My friend the sergeant was one of those who ran into it, but there was a quick burst of machine-gun fire and he came reeling out clutching his shoulder. Someone shouted at him and he staggered back towards the tanks. Goldsworthy and I jumped out and lifted him on to the engine covers. The mortaring had started again by this time so we got him into the turret, gave him a shot of morphine in the back of his hand and marked the time and date in blue crayon on his forehead. It looked to be a clean wound, the bullet having passed through his shoulder area.

Then came the message for the attack to stop and for us all to withdraw to the entrance of the village again. We were furious, as we felt that we had beaten the enemy and that within a few minutes would have the centre of the village and the crossroads under our total control. Despite a plea by the Queens company commander the order was not rescinded and a disconsolate little force returned to settle into positions just short of the village itself. 'No bloody fortune for me this time,' said the wounded sergeant, as we put him into the medical half-track!

The day had begun by being rather misty and overcast, but by midday as we withdrew it was sunny and warm. The tanks and infantry having been settled into their new positions, we brewed up and, although the turrets remained manned, half of each crew relaxed while I sat on the back of my tank with the Company Commander from the Queens. We were looking out to the east of Loon-op-Zand over a huge open meadow which was about half a mile across, ending in a belt of woodland which ran along the main east–west road out of the village. We saw activity to our right rear and suddenly heard the skirl of bagpipes. To our astonishment two companies of the Gordon Highlanders appeared in extended order and almost marched across the meadows towards the main road. Behind them was their piper, followed by their colonel with a walking stick and presumably the adjutant and other HQ staff, and behind them again a further company also in extended order. There were a few mortar bombs dropping in the area of the advance and any casualties were picked up by stretcher bearers. In a matter of minutes, or so it seemed, they disappeared into the trees to our left and we heard small arms fire which gradually died away. There was an air of unreality about the whole episode and I felt that I had been watching a battle in the Peninsular War rather than an infantry attack mounted in 1944.

The squadron went into regimental reserve later in the day and we spent the next few days in the small town of Dongen, where we were treated as liberators and enjoyed the comfort of good billets and the approbation of the inhabitants. It was a refreshing break and we rather resented being moved out to Sprang, which was further north closer to the Maas, and near the village of Waalwijk. As we arrived in the village we were greeted by the most almighty 'stonk' from the German guns. An accolade which was not appreciated and which, thank goodness, was not repeated during the ten days in which we stayed there. Sprang had suffered during the battles and was badly damaged, but despite this we were all lodged under cover in comparative comfort and greatly appreciated the hospitality which the local people offered. It was there that for the first time I realised the affinity between the Dutch language and a broad Scottish accent. Bill Pritchard's wireless operator was a Glaswegian and never ceased to let us know it. He could converse with the locals in their language. 'Church' was 'Kirk', and 'Awa to the hoose' was like their 'Aweg t'huis', and so on. He obtained eggs and other food for us without any difficulty.

Little happened to A Squadron during this stay, but we did join the whole regiment in an unusual effort in support of the 51st Highland Division. They were to attack two villages south of the river which were still under the control of the enemy. The division was short of artillery, so the regiment lined up by squadrons, and behind each tank or group of tanks was a three ton lorry full of HE shells. We were given a compass bearing, lined up the guns, and raised them to maximum elevation and then blazed away for about half an hour. The target villages were soon a mass of smoke and we were thanked afterwards for our 'extremely effective' fire, which had helped the infantry greatly in their attack.

Another memory of the battles in this area concerned a grave error of judgement by Tony Hind and me. It had been a filthy wet day and we arrived in leaguer soaked to the skin with no billets anywhere nearby. Tony noticed an old wooden hen house in a field so we walked over to it, looked inside and found that it was dry and fairly clean with no sign of hens. Feeling rather clever we collected our bedding rolls, lay them on the floor and eventually settled down for the night. Within a couple of hours we both woke up scratching and covered in bites. We were crawling with red mites which must have infested the hut. I got no sympathy from my crew, and they seemed quite reluctant to let me travel with them the next day.

Soon after this we were ordered south to the Belgian town of Maeseyck, situated on the west bank of the Maas. It was a long haul, some 100 miles covered in one day. It is illustrative of the new flexibility within the British Zone, that such distances could be covered with such speed. During one of the stages of this move, I was acting as lead tank and we were roaring along the centre of a typical cambered, cobbled, dead straight road. I suppose that we were travelling about 20mph, when a gaggle of Dutch men and women mounted on their bicycles suddenly rounded the corner about 200 yards ahead of us. On seeing our tank, they stopped and began waving happily to us, but before I could respond, out of the corner of my eye, I caught sight of a black elliptical object emerging at high speed from the right-hand side of our tank. It was hurtling straight at the Dutch cyclists, who scattered in all directions, some across the road, others into the ditch. One of the thick rubber tyres, which are sweated on to each of the suspension wheels on the Cromwell, had detached itself. It must have weighed a good 50–60lb and was travelling like a slingshot at about 60mph! Luckily nobody was hurt and it was all taken in good part, but it was a sick-making moment.

We reached Maeseyck as evening fell and to our delight found ourselves billeted in the town itself. Squadron orders that evening stressed the need for care, as the town was reported to be full of spies.

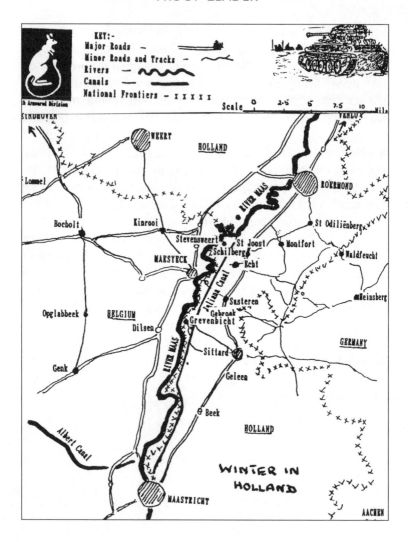

KEY:-
Major Roads —
Minor Roads and Tracks —
Rivers —
Canals —
National Frontiers — x x x x x

Scale 0   2.5   5   7.5   10   Miles

WINTER IN HOLLAND

NINE

The Maas, Dutch Winter

We arrived in Maeseyck on 11 November, Armistice Day. It was not a very exciting town in which to be billeted and, although we made the best of it, I personally never felt very welcome there. Our squadron Officers' Mess was set up in a café on the main street. There were shops on either side of us, but they were almost empty of goods. My billet was about 400 yards away, in a small house towards the railway station, and I was allocated a tiny front room overlooking the road. My 'landlady' was preoccupied with her family and her own problems so, although my occasional gift of food was welcomed, we didn't have much in common. My troop were billeted in houses around the same area and, as usual, dug themselves in well and made themselves very comfortable. We anticipated a long rest when we reached Maeseyck and were startled to find that we were to live in houses but continue to fight battles. As Tony said, 'Makes you feel as if you're in the RAF!' We were also subjected to shelling, but luckily it never seemed to be in our immediate vicinity.

The immediate problem facing the British Army at the time was the capture of all the ground up to the River Maas, so as to give us a clear jumping off point for the invasion of Germany, the previous two months' battles having cleared the Germans from Holland in the north and west. Our division was to be responsible for the area close to

Maeseyck and our initial task was to capture the Panheel lock on the Wessem canal. This lay beyond the villages of Thorn and Wessem about five miles to the north of the town. The canal itself ran between high banks, and the enemy were well entrenched there with a good field of fire. It was wet country, horrible for tanks. A Squadron's role in this battle was of a minor nature. On 14 November we went to a cement works which lay between two villages. Our action was to be diversionary, we laid smoke and we shot at any target we could see, or imagined we could see. I did not find it a very stimulating day and was very happy to come home to bed. B and C Squadrons had a more energetic battle and their involvement continued for several days.

I woke up next morning with a raging toothache. Tony was delighted – memories of Normandy but alas no Calvados – and took me to the field dental unit which was situated on the top of a small hill. This unit was tented but with the Red Crosses well displayed. The front flaps of the dentist's surgery were open and looked out over the ground which we had fought over on the previous day. It was extraordinary to lie back in the chair and watch the other squadrons still deploying in the area. The dentist was highly skilled and removed a nerve from one of my teeth. I have never had any further trouble from it.

After this brief sortie, life settled down and we set out to find our own enjoyment in and around Maeseyck. Many people found girl friends there, there were some dances for the soldiers, and there was a lot of drinking and general high jinks. Block leave was granted to enable as many as possible to get back to Brussels. Alan Howard was on duty at a dance one night when a number of soldiers from another regiment, who were billeted near us, set about him and he ended up in hospital. Unfortunately he did not return for several weeks and Corporal Arnold was posted as the replacement to my troop. He was a regular soldier, always immaculately turned out, with highly polished boots. I think, initially anyway, he found the troop to be a little unconventional.

We visited each others' messes, especially that of B Squadron which was not far from us, and very upmarket in terms of accommodation. Richard Dill of that squadron was a great friend both of mine and of Tony Hind, and we had a lot of fun together. I met a girl there who gave me her photograph, her name was Tilly, but I can't actually remember any social occasion which I attended with her. On the back of the photo it says, 'Vous souvenez vous de cette jeune fille?' And I don't, so obviously she didn't make much of an impression!

The two senior captains in our mess were, in my eyes, old and experienced and they used to regale me with tales of their historic conquests that left me gasping. I wrote a series of couplets about each of them which they found amusing, I only remember two of them:

> Jack, with tache and eyes that riveted,
> Took girls who fidgeted,
> And showed them how to stop it!

and about Bob – I have forgotten it except for:

> Sleek black hair well buttered back,
> With Trumper's most expensive tack,

which actually described him quite well.

The date of my twenty-first birthday was 1 December 1944 and we had planned a weekend of celebrations which would have demolished my slender savings. The actual day fell on a Friday so there was plenty of scope. With Tony's imaginative help we laid on a series of parties starting with a thrash in our own mess. However, on Thursday night we received preliminary orders to leave Maeseyck, packed up the tanks on the Friday and departed for Maastricht on Saturday morning, 2 December. Unfortunately, therefore, my party was deferred.

It was a journey of some 30 miles down to Maastricht, and then back up the other side of the Maas to Papenhoven. We travelled on a minor road alongside the Juliana canal. When we reached the dispersal point I realised that we were only three miles from Maeseyck, but on the opposite side of the river. The bridge at Maeseyck was not replaced until January 1945. It was bitterly cold and the snow began as we arrived. To my initial horror I was told that our role was to be that of infantry, and our tanks were to remain in the rear area. We then all went out in squadron transport to the village of Gebroek where I was allocated a few semi-demolished houses on the forward edge of the village, shown where the enemy were, and told to set up a defensive position. An hour or so later a young officer whom I knew arrived from the Rifle Brigade and he told us all about infantry patrols, standing patrols, siting Bren guns on a fixed line and a variety of other helpful hints. I felt quite confident that we would acquit ourselves well, although facing us, 500 yards away in and around Bakenhoven, was a German parachute regiment and they were very tough indeed.

I was still coming to terms with the idea of being a 'real soldier', as my Rifle Brigade friend had informed me, when I woke up in the night with a raging temperature and on 5 December, was removed by ambulance to the forward hospital in Eindhoven. I had a severe attack of sinusitis, coupled with a virus infection. I was quite delirious for a few days and remember little. The hospital was in a large school building and when my temperature had subsided, I was sent down to a tented area where an orderly stuck a stick with cotton wool on it, up my nose, handed me a wash basin and told me that I would be called into the operating area when

the anaesthetic had worked. Apparently the wool was soaked in cocaine. The whole procedure was very crude and I didn't enjoy it much.

When I returned to my bed, feeling pretty shaky, I found Colonel Cuthie standing there. We exchanged a few pleasantries, during the course of which he said that he understood that my belated twenty-first birthday party had been a great success, but what a pity that I hadn't been there to enjoy it! He then told me that I had been awarded an immediate Military Cross for my leadership during the battle for Doornhoek back in October. He congratulated me, handed me a personal letter of congratulations from the divisional commander, General Lyne, which also contained a piece of the medal ribbon, and then left. I was stunned at the news, elated that I had received such an honour, and overwhelmed by the congratulations of the other patients. Somebody produced a bottle of scotch, one of the nurses sewed the ribbon on to my battledress and we had a bit of a party in the ward.

I was discharged on 16 December and returned to find that the squadron had moved in my absence and were now billeted in houses around Grevenbicht, a village adjoining Papenhoven. Snow was falling and the temperature had dropped dramatically during my few days away. I felt most embarrassed to be walking about with my brand new medal ribbon, very conscious that a number of the others deserved it more than I did, and aware that if it had not been for the support of my troop I wouldn't have had a medal anyway. In fact my first job on returning was to arrange a troop party to celebrate 'their' medal, and we achieved this in some style in a café in Grevenbicht. Bill Pritchard gave a speech which made the troop's proprietary claim to the medal quite clear, and then proposed a toast, and we all got rather drunk. It was a good party. On returning to my billet, the comfortable, but to me middle-aged, lady of the house – she must have been quite thirty! – came into my bedroom and sat on the edge on my bed in her dressing gown. Looking back on it now, I realise that she was offering to complete my evening in the traditional way. It went right over my head and she must have left for her own room somewhat astonished at my naivety. Next day I was posted back to Brussels for a course on mine clearance at the divisional battle school.

Brussels this time was fun. I was with a batch of spirited young officers, we worked quite hard during the day but we were all determined to enjoy ourselves in the evenings. Life centred around the Officers' Club in the Rue de la Loi, sited in the old British Embassy; 'Le Jockey Club', a nightspot in the Avenue Louise; and the 'Eye' Club for the guards officers in the Boulevard Anspach. Our evenings usually began at the Officers' Club where we were fairly uninhibited, but where senior officers were very understanding of our high spirits. The entrance hall to the club was marbled and above it was a mezzanine floor with wrought iron railings around it, from which one could look down into the hall beneath. We favoured this spot for our parties as it dominated the entrance. It was there that we developed a highly dangerous para-jump game. One of us was nominated as a caller and as our name was called, so we ran to the railing, vaulted over it and dropped 12–15 feet on to the marble floor below. The caller used to try to select suitably important senior officers to be at the landing point at the time, and it was a matter of great skill to twist as one took off and just avoid them on landing. There were no casualties, to my knowledge.

The main bar of the club was a massive wooden structure, circular and undercut with a brass foot rail running around the circumference. We discovered that there was room for a man to crawl around the bar behind this without being seen from above. Simultaneous to that discovery, the cult of the 'hot foot' had been resuscitated. This entailed inserting a match into the welt of a man's shoe, sulphur end foremost, lighting the wooden end and retiring to a safe distance to watch the results. These could be quite startling. The people sitting round the bar were very boring one evening, and Patrick Hartwright and I felt that things needed livening up. We ducked under the bar and, crawling round it, managed to insert matches into eight shoes without being detected. We timed our lighting to a tee and withdrew discreetly from the ends to await results, which were almost instantaneous. Eight shouts of pain, eight shoes wrenched off, and general consternation all around. We were never caught.

We returned to the regiment in time for Christmas and found things much as we had left them, except that the snow was even deeper and it was bitterly cold. I was glad to be back with the troop and found that we were to take over a sector of the front in a small village near Holtum, acting in support of the Rifle Brigade. We were still in the role of infantry. The headquarters of I Company of the Rifle Brigade occupied a cellar in the centre of the village. As we arrived, two days before Christmas, a mortar 'stonk' was in progress, and interspersed with the shrapnel bombs were canisters carrying propaganda leaflets. These leaflets were a source of joy to us all, depicting as they did American soldiers and British girls in highly compromising positions under the headline, 'Yanks living it up with your wife Tommy, while you lose your life on the western front. Go home.' The drawings were crude enough to be good for a laugh. Tragically, as I was making my way to see the company commander on Christmas Eve, one of these canisters fell directly into the mouth of his dug-out, killing him instantly. It was a sad start to Christmas as he was a good friend to us all.

My particular responsibility was to watch a quadrant on the north east side of the village, which included the road to Susteren. The sector contained the church, a large pig farm and a number of empty houses. There were no civilians in the village and even the animals had been evacuated. I sited my headquarters in a small deserted farmhouse with a well furnished, carpeted kitchen in which we could get reasonably warm. At the side was a narrow sheltered yard which was perfect for my scout-car. It was still bitterly cold and we were all very bored. We were forbidden to light proper fires as the smoke would have divulged our exact location; the mortaring was uncommonly accurate and the Germans were occupying several of the houses further down the road but on the outskirts of the village. We were still facing a German parachute regiment at the time and it was unwise to take risks.

Those who were not on guard duty spent a great deal of their spare time in their bedding rolls keeping warm. While I shared their boredom, I was incapable of 'switching off' in the way that all British soldiers seem to be able to do, and I roamed about the village looking into all the houses and trying to find better positions. I must also admit that I was ever hopeful of finding some bottles of the excellent preserves that the Dutch seemed to manage to put away in their cellars, despite the rationing and general hardship. I was unlucky in the latter, but I did find a rather scrawny hen, the sole occupant of a fine house in the centre of the village. I failed to catch her, but I ensured that the door was tightly shut, and dispatched a couple of soldiers to see that she was captured before the Rifle Brigade located her. They brought her in, clucking indignantly and clearly proclaiming her rights as an ally. However it was Christmas Eve, and chicken was very much on the menu for those lucky enough to find one. The only problem was that no one had ever wrung a chicken's neck before, and not one of us fancied doing it. Eventually, Goldsmith volunteered; he was a cockney and rarely at a loss. He took the hen out into the yard where there was a chopping block and, closing his eyes, he took an enormous swipe at her, missing completely, but certainly destroying any misplaced confidence that she might have had in him. She burst out of his hand and, hotly pursued by Goldsmith and his chopper, dashed around the yard to the rousing cheers of us all. I would like to be able to say that she escaped the final blow and lived to tell her chicks of the experience, but eventually she was cornered and dispatched. She did add some flavour to our stew on Christmas Day, so she did not die in vain.

As darkness fell that night, despite the circumstances, a sense of the spirit of Christmas seemed to come over us. Everyone became wrapped up in his own thoughts and memories and we were all unusually silent. There is an indefinable beauty about the concept of Christmas, peace and the Christ child, which defies the circumstances and imparts joy and goodwill to us all wherever we may be. Late that evening as I went round the sentries with Bill Pritchard, we heard the sound of singing coming from the German lines. We didn't recognise any of the tunes but found it strangely moving. Initially we thought that it was another propaganda broadcast coming over loudspeakers some distance from our lines. However, when we reached our foremost position we could hear it more clearly and it was definitely their front line troops. This, on the face of it, was totally out of character as they were a very tough crowd indeed, and shows how Christmas affects everyone. We did not attempt to sing to them.

There was no activity in our sector that night or indeed on Christmas Day itself, no exchange of fire and no obvious movement by either side, although we did not relax our vigilance. The day itself was one of clear blue skies, some warmth in the sun if you could get out of the wind, but still with the frozen white landscape all around us. We were visited by 'Jumbo' Phillips, who was commanding in Colonel Cuthie's absence, and various other friends dropped in for a drink and a talk. I released some chaps so that they could attend a church carol service at regimental HQ, but by midday we were all hard at it, happily consuming the food and drink that we had managed to collect. I visited each location and had a drink, so was feeling very good by the time I returned to my billet. My crew had concocted a splendid spread out of the choicest tins from the ration packs, hoarded during the past weeks. I had a special passion for the treacle puddings and they had a whole one for me, as well as Christmas pudding and a vast plate of stew and vegetables. We all had gargantuan appetites, so little was wasted.

Having downed the meal I felt in need of some exercise; no one else seemed at all interested, especially when I announced that I wanted to visit the church as it was Christmas Day. There had been no Mass available for us as we were rather outlying. There was a fine church in my sector which I had visited once before to see if it was suitable as a lookout post. When I got there I found the side door ajar so I pushed it open and entered. I was quite surprised at the size of the building, bearing in mind that it wasn't a very large village. The interior was stark, a giant crucifix hung over the high altar, there was no sanctuary lamp and the atmosphere was not very prayerful. I went into the sacristy which had been stripped of all the vestments, so evidently the evacuation had been very orderly, and then returned to the dark and gloomy nave.

As I walked towards the back of the church, I noticed an organ loft with tiers of choir stalls behind it. Access to this was by a circular staircase in the tower, so I climbed up the stairs and at the top found a large and very impressive organ. I have always been fascinated by organs, and I sat on the stool in front of it and experimented with the various stops and pedals. There was no electricity in the village so I could not actually play a tune, but simulating the chords and imagining the power of the great pipes was satisfying. I amused myself doing this for some time and then heard footsteps on the stairs, so I adopted my most professional stance ready to impress whichever member of my troop appeared round the door. When the person appeared it wasn't a member of my troop at all, and I was stunned to see a young German officer in his long grey greatcoat and peaked cap. He couldn't have been any older than I was and for a brief second, which seemed an eternity, we both looked at each other in horror. Then suddenly he flung himself down the stairwell, and as I rushed to the edge of the loft I could hear the great clatter of his feet as he half fell down the stairs themselves. I did not see him emerge in the nave, so I spent a very uncomfortable time trying to make up my mind whether he was waiting at the back of the church with his gun at the ready, or whether he had gone. Eventually I regained my composure, took off my shoes and eased my way silently down the stairs with my back pressed nervously against the wall. To my relief there was nobody there, but I did notice for the first time a small door at the rear of the tower. This was open, so I concluded that my friend had gone out that way. On investigation I discovered that this small doorway looked straight out towards the German lines, and it was a far better observation point than any of the ones which I had chosen. We occupied the church immediately, and sited a post behind the cemetery wall adjacent to the doorway.

I often wonder whether the German officer, like me, had decided to come into the church for a little privacy at Christmastide. Had he panicked and run out of the church or had he, in that short moment when we faced each other, felt revulsion at the idea of the sort of personal killing that this type of encounter would have engendered? Perhaps he had no weapon with him? I shall never know. Personally speaking I never gained any satisfaction from the act of killing. I acted more in the spirit of self-preservation than in a determined effort to kill the enemy. In a way I felt apologetic when I either pressed the trigger or caused it to be pressed. Warfare to me was a type of 'super wide-game' such as we played at school, but it had a high degree of risk and certain irreversible consequences. I found myself being allocated targets to achieve and I tried to achieve these without loss of life on my side and hopefully with a minimum loss of life on that of the enemy. The only time when I had felt a strong urge to kill was when we faced the SS Panzer divisions, who behaved so wickedly at the time of the breakout from France. Anyway, whatever may have been the German's motives, I felt that I had received a very wonderful Christmas gift.

Boxing Day brought a return of hostilities, and the adjacent village of Gebroek, which I knew well from previous engagements, was captured by the Germans. They took the 11th Hussars by surprise and brewed up a number of their vehicles. After a splendid artillery bombardment, Frank Saxby's troop went in and cleared the village again. It was a sharp but punishing engagement and it brought us back to the realities of war. We stayed in Gebroek with our friends in the Rifle Brigade for two weeks, celebrated the New Year well, and then woke up witness to the tremendous air effort which the Germans mounted at that time in support of their Ardennes offensive. It was the first time that I had seen any number of enemy aircraft in the sky and the general activity was most stimulating. We watched the dog-fights going on above us and were thankful that the bombing and machine-gunning were not directed at us. Later in the day we were astonished to see large numbers of V1 bombs going over our positions. They could not have been launched from far away as they were extremely low. We were told that their target point was the port of Antwerp. Initially we tried to shoot them down with machine-gun fire or with our Sten guns, but when someone succeeded we heard the subsequent explosion in our echelon lines so we desisted. A troop on our left managed to turn one which sailed joyfully back towards the Reich. We all cheered at that.

One of the most remarkable things about the winter of 1944 in the south of Limburg was the sheer, almost unbelievable, harshness of the weather. Our English winter is, relatively speaking, mild and we are not accustomed to the fierce biting winds which blow consistently for weeks, freezing still further a land already thickly covered with snow and ice. I travelled in the command seat of a Humber scout-car as for a time I was acting as mines adviser to the regiment, having been on the course in Brussels, and thus spent my life visiting individual troops in their defence positions which were spread over a fairly wide area. It was too cold to see without goggles and yet impossible to wear them, as they froze on to your nose. If you took them off, in order to have a clear view, your eyes filled with tears, which either froze to your face or failing that, your eyelids froze shut. It was all very uncomfortable. Luckily the regimental doctor shared a requisitioned house with our squadron HQ and seeing my plight, he gave me a large tin of neat lanolin which I spread liberally over every exposed portion of my anatomy. This did not contribute to my cleanliness but did afford protection. It played havoc with the fur collar of my beloved American flying jacket, but then, who cared as long as one could stay warm and free from frost-burn. My dress lacked formality, warmth was all. I wore pyjamas under my underclothes, a thick shirt and sweater, corduroy trousers and that marvellous fur-collared American jacket, acquired from 101 Airborne while we were in St Oedenrode.

In our new role as infantrymen, part of the squadron was deployed in slit trenches covering the tow path along the banks of a canal. The weather conditions were such that it was still practically impossible for tanks to operate. As troop leader of 3 Troop, I had a particular affinity with the men in that troop, and visited them whenever possible. I was on my rounds one crystal, starlit night as they manned a forward post on the western side of the canal, just to the south of Wetteren Lock. At the point where we had sited their post, the canal turned slightly to the right and thus they were shielded from the direct enfilade fire of anyone firing straight down the towpath. We had been told that the German forward positions were about 500 yards to our front, adjacent to the lock itself. We had not heard anything of them since we had taken over two nights before, and although we had been forbidden to reconnoitre forward along the canal towpath, it was unsettling for everyone to be in doubt as to the exact dispositions of the enemy.

During this particular routine night round, I left the post, scrambled down the canal bank to the edge of the ice, which was some two or three feet thick, and then slid down the ice itself towards the centre of the canal. The water level had dropped substantially, and the ice had stretched to accommodate this, forming a concave surface with a fall in the centre of some two or three feet. I noticed that the ice at the edges was stable, smooth and regular, despite the slope. I remember standing there quietly enjoying the incredible peace of the night and the marvellous deep soft blue-black light which enveloped the whole countryside and gave it a strange sort of warmth. Suddenly I became aware of someone standing on the bank behind me and was very relieved to find that it was Alan Howard, who, wondering where I had gone to, had come quietly along the edge of the ice to look for me. He remarked on the difficulty of detecting somebody when they were actually on the ice as they were always below you, owing to the fall in the water level.

We walked back to the post together and I suddenly saw how easy it would be to slip on a pair of the long steel Dutch skates with their wooden tops and leather straps, and using the slope on the ice, reach the lock itself without any chance of detection. It was an exciting idea, it didn't break any of the stringent rules as I would not actually be advancing up the towpath, and yet it was a way of trying to establish whether the Germans had left. I slipped back to the main troop dug-outs and roused one of the younger sergeants. There were plenty of Dutch skates in the various houses which we occupied. We had been out skating together during the week and I knew he was competent. What did he think of the idea? 'Great,' he said. Clearly he felt that anything was better than the awful boredom of sitting in the freezing cold doing nothing.

We collected our skates and walked quietly back to the lookout post. It was about 0200hrs, absolute stillness everywhere, and the world seemed to be at total peace. We told Alan Howard of our intentions, 'Bloody crazy,' he said, but then he never did mince matters. He alerted the whole post and they manned their guns, just in case. We were all a little excited at the prospect of activity and with some warm good wishes and a few unrepeatable asides, we slipped down to the canal and put on our skates. First we did a few practice swoops up and down the ice wall and then when we were both satisfied that we could manage the not very difficult motion necessary to progress almost noiselessly along the edge of the canal, we set off and rounded the corner. My companion stationed himself about twenty yards behind me.

It was very exhilarating, progress was fast and very easy, we hardly had to move the skates at all, simply keep the feet together and swoop up and down in an S pattern, using the slope to give the necessary power. Looking back on it forty years later I realise how stupid and irresponsible it was for me to have done such a thing, but at the time it seemed a marvellous way to gain information at little risk. All went well and the sound of water rushing down the face of the Lock-gates grew louder. I could see the lock gates ahead but it was impossible to judge distance and it was difficult to divine exactly how far we had progressed. Suddenly I found myself gaining speed and sliding down the sloping edge of the ice face into total darkness. Too late I realised that I had actually arrived at the pool at the base of the lock gates. I struggled to turn into the bank but the ice had cracked and fragmented at this point and it was too sheer to permit me to climb it. I must have shouted, as the sergeant told me later that although he couldn't see me he had heard my shout and had flung himself down on to the ice and slid to a stop in shallow water. In desperation, I threw myself to the left towards the centre of the canal, hoping that the ice would bear me, although by this time I was up to my knees in water. Luck was on my side; the ice was solid beneath the water, I completed the circle and, wet and shaken, I managed to clamber back to the edge and safety.

We met up at the edge, both shivering with cold and both very relieved that we had escaped with nothing worse than a wetting. It was clear that we could not go forward as we could now see the water gushing out of the centre vents of the lock above us. I was just wondering whether we should take off the skates and climb the canal bank, when suddenly a bright light shone out on to the tow path just above us and then all hell was let lose, with Schmeissers going off in all directions. Tracer bullets whistled over our heads and it suddenly became imperative not to be there. It is arguable as to which of us passed the post first. There were witnesses who swore that we were skating so fast we overtook the machine gun bullets sweeping down the canal; some gave the sergeant a win on points but I am convinced that the Olympic skating speed record was surpassed by the pair of us. It is said that fear gives a man wings; well, we came very close to growing them that night.

We both shot round the corner to safety, eventually stopping about 200 yards beyond the post itself. We were totally winded and we sat together, laughing, panting and gasping for breath. It was Alan Howard's moment. He climbed down to us and told me that he had contacted squadron HQ. My heart sank. He then said that he had reported enemy activity ahead against unknown targets, adding that as the fire was not apparently directed at his post, he had not fired back as he thought it best to protect the precise location of our position. He added that his patrol would appreciate rum as soon as practical. The acceptable price of silence! That was the first and the last time that I undertook a patrol on the ice on skates, although a few days later I had further trouble on the ice.

Two troops of the squadron occupied a farm in the central sector of the regimental front. It comprised a substantial farmhouse, a range of outbuildings and, at the rear, a large vegetable garden. This overlooked the fields at the back and was bordered by a retaining wall some six feet in height. At the base of this wall, a narrow grass strip abutted the edge of a moat, which at that point was about 30 feet wide. The water extended for quite a long way in each direction and it was well-reeded especially on the far bank. Beyond the reeds lay an orchard of mature trees and somewhere behind this, the German front line. One evening, while I was duty officer, there was a great deal of activity immediately to our left, with frequent bursts of machine gun fire, the explosion of hand grenades and star shells bursting overhead. I stood the troops to until it came to an end, as it seemed probable that an enemy patrol was moving along the squadron front. We were all highly amused when word came down through the regimental net, that 'Goon' Gadsby, a young officer who was notorious for his misadventures, had spent some hours laying trip flares and anti-personnel mines to his troop front, and then walked back through one of them, setting them off. His troop fought a gallant rearguard action with a non-existent enemy. That particular party finished at about 2200hrs and there was no response from the Germans.

Bill Pritchard and I sat on the retaining wall with our feet dangling over the edge, looking out across the frozen moat, and listening in the quiet of the night to the rumble of the supply wagons behind the German lines. They still used a great deal of horse transport, as we had seen during the breakout from Normandy, and it had its own distinctive noise. The orchard in front of us was thick with snow, but the trees were planted very close together and the shadows were impenetrable. After a little while we thought that we had heard a faint noise coming from the direction of the trees, but we were unable to see anything from where we were sitting. We discussed the matter and, thinking that it was probably an animal, I decided to cross the ice to the bank on the far side and take a closer look. Bill Pritchard alerted the sentries as to our intended movements and instructed them not to fire unless one of us called for it or if they saw movement inside the orchard itself. We then slipped silently down the face of the wall, he staying on the farm bank to give me some close cover. I stretched out on the ice on my stomach, then wriggled forward through the reeds and pulled myself across the ice to the other bank. It was quiet and there was an air of stillness everywhere. I found a gap where the reeds had been beaten down, probably a drinking place for the cattle, and lay there for a moment, then hearing no noises, I drew my revolver and crawled on to the slope of the snow-covered bank which rose about two feet above me. I started to rise to my knees in order to peer over the top, when some instinct caused me to delay.

A moment later I heard movement to my right. It was quite faint but unmistakably the sound of metal or of some object hitting against another. I slipped back on to my stomach and listened intently. After what seemed an age but was probably only a few seconds I heard it again but this time it was very much closer and sounded like human beings. I realised that it was probably a German patrol and I had been caught wrong-footed. If I went back over the ice I would be seen immediately, while if I stayed where I was, although I had some concealment, I could be caught in the crossfire. It was an unhappy position to be in, but before I had any opportunity to make a positive decision I found myself looking directly into the face of a huge, panting Alsatian dog, its breath positively smoking in the cold night air. It was on top of the bank and attached to it was a German soldier. It was one of the dogs which the Germans had trained for mine detection. Following the dog handler was a patrol of four soldiers.

Looking back on it, it really was sheer pantomime, as the dog totally ignored me and continued on its way, presumably carrying out with German thoroughness the task for which it had been trained. Neither the handler nor the patrol noticed me as I lay there on the bank, although they were clearly visible to me. I can only presume that the reeds had broken up my shape and I was hidden to those people standing above me. I lay still for several minutes in case there were more patrols, then, hearing nothing, I cautiously worked my way up the bank. I could just make out the dim figures to my left as they disappeared into the shadow of the orchard. I raced back over the ice to call down some fire and found, to my astonishment, neither Bill Pritchard nor the sentries on duty had heard or seen anything. I could not fix the point of entry into the orchard with any accuracy so, on balance, I decided to let them depart in peace. After which, noting the clear air of disbelief registered by my soldiery, I retired to my bedding roll and slept until first light and stand-to. Next day, when we had stood down, and breakfast was being prepared, there being no sign of enemy activity, I crossed over the ice again with Bill Pritchard and Smith, my wireless operator, to check for tracks on the far bank. We found the tracks of two dogs and a handler – apparently they operated in tandem – and the rather more confused tracks of several men. I felt vindicated but rather rueful that I had not shown more aggression under the circumstances.

Shortly after this I suffered another bout of stomach trouble and was sent back to hospital for investigation. I found myself in a girls' school in Ghent which had been adapted as a base hospital. I was 'walking wounded' and during the second day I was visited by a charming Belgian lady, Madame de Smet, and her equally nice daughter, Poupette. They invited me to visit them at their house which was near at hand. I met the whole of their family and became very fond of them all. I was returned to the regiment after five short days, but from this brief meeting has come a lifelong attachment to the de Smet family.

TEN

St Joost, Hospital in England

During the early days of January we were ordered to whitewash the armoured vehicles. It was a messy business, but a cheap and fairly effective form of camouflage. The German offensive in the Ardennes had been halted, and in that sector they were in full retreat. It was logical therefore to think that we too would soon mount an offensive to clear all German troops out of the area to the west of the River Rhine so that the final thrust into Germany could be made. I was spending much of my day in a Humber scout-car at this time, acting temporarily as squadron second captain. The cold was still knife-like in its intensity; moving in open vehicles such as a scout-car, where one's head was permanently out of the turret facing a keen wind, was painful in the extreme. Despite the protective covering of lanolin my nose and eyes suffered and were very raw. I was not alone.

The division were back in their tanks again as the ground was like concrete under the snow, and armoured vehicles could move with impunity over areas previously so marshy as to be impassable to them. There was, in fact, a great deal of troop movement, and wherever I went rumour of action was rife. It was no surprise therefore when on 17 January John Gwynne told us to get the squadron ready to move. My copy of the 'Operation Order No. 15' was issued on that day. It looked routine, with the regiment advancing two squadrons up, C Squadron astride the main road towards

181

Linne and A Squadron alongside them on their right, making between them a small pincer movement to capture Montfort, some five miles to our north-west. The recce troop were given a role out on our west flank.

Two days earlier I had handed my troop over to Dallas Barnes, who had rejoined the squadron. It would be untrue to say that I was happy to do this, and I disliked the idea of the troop going into action without me. I was jealous of their safety and my record. We had not lost a man through enemy action in the campaign and I didn't want that to happen now. I knew that Bill Pritchard was on edge as a result of the change, but there was nothing I could do to ease the situation. The order to move came on 20 January. We moved off towards the start line in the late morning and passed through Schilberg, which had been flattened. At about midday we met up with John, who had selected an assembly position on the west side of the Schilberg–St Joost road, about one mile short of St Joost itself. We pulled the tanks off the road and lined up along the hedge. There was a tremendous amount of firing going on in the whole area, especially from the direction of St Joost. In fact, shortly there was so much shot and shell flying around that the order was given for all personnel to remain in their tanks.

In the early afternoon, John called me over to his tank and said that he wanted to discuss with me the part that the squadron was to play in this battle. We then walked across the field to the road, which was raised about two feet above the surrounding fields, and proceeded to pace up and down a stretch, perhaps 100 yards long, talking. I found it difficult to concentrate on his conversation! It was as if we were walking across the front of the firing point on a tank-cum-infantry gunnery range with all arms firing. Shots were whistling past us, over us, and ricocheting off the road. It was sheer madness, and yet I knew that I couldn't lose face by suggesting to this tough fearless little man that our talk would be more meaningful if held in the shelter of one of the tanks. It gave me some idea of the type of courage demanded of all ranks in the battles of the Napoleonic War – Waterloo for instance. It would be wrong to say that I was frightened, in fact I experienced a kind of exhilaration, but even at the time it struck me that we were 'pushing our luck a bit'. It was not necessary to impress the squadron at this stage of the campaign and in any event, as Corporal Howard said later, 'You must be bloody mad!'

It appeared that heavy resistance had been encountered at St Joost, and as a result B Squadron had been selected to investigate, much to John's annoyance as he wanted the task for his squadron. However, we had been ordered to continue to probe out to the west of the Hingen–St Joost road, and Richard Anstey's troop plus an element of the recce troop went up through Hingen itself. They crossed the brook there and, as they broke into the open country, they were fired on by anti-tank guns, a Honey tank from the recce troop was destroyed and they were unable to make further progress. Meanwhile the battle in St Joost itself became fiercer and fiercer. It was a desperate struggle between first-class British troops and one of the toughest of the German parachute regiments, 'Hubners'. Eventually, my squadron was ordered to deploy and cover the road in case any of the German troops managed to slip through. Darkness fell and we passed a night of alarms, dozing in our vehicles. The battle continued into the night and to add to our general discomfort it snowed heavily again.

Early on the morning of 21 January, another attack was mounted on St Joost. Once again B Squadron, under the command of Wingate Charlton, fought with great gallantry in support of the infantry. The morning was made even more difficult by the thick fog which reduced visibility to less than 100 yards. Richard Anstey and Dallas Barnes were ordered to take their two troops, retrace the route of the previous day and find a way round St Joost, to outflank it from the east. I was very worked up about 'my troop' going into action under another officer and as they left, I asked permission to accompany them in the scout-car. This was refused, but, a little later, I was sent to the bridge in Hingen to act as a forward wireless link. The tanks clattered off into the dense fog and all went well for some minutes and then I heard Richard shout over the wireless, 'Two SPs to our front – engaging', and at the same time I heard the crack of three shots from tank guns. This was followed by a series of shots, then silence. As I moved forward in the scout-car, Richard's voice came up on the wireless to report that two of his tanks had been knocked out, followed immediately by Dallas, who had lost one. They were told to return to the area of the bridge where I was waiting.

Dallas came back first, carrying the crew of his Sherman Firefly on his engine covers. Apparently, as they approached some farm buildings, the fog rolled back momentarily and three German self- propelled guns appeared on their left flank. He turned to engage, driving towards the buildings for cover, when a glancing shot hit his Firefly, equipped with a 17-pdr gun; it then ran into a farm building and crashed through the floor into the cellar. Apart from bruises, no one was hurt. Richard was short of two crew members, both of whom had been killed. The fog only lifted for a matter of seconds and the Germans got away unscathed. Clearly advance under those conditions was impractical and the squadron were told to sit tight until the fog situation improved. I then returned to the squadron HQ with the survivors.

By one o'clock the fog had started to lift a little, and John was worried about the undamaged tank which had been abandoned. There had been no sight or sound of enemy in the area and I suggested taking the scout-car, which was very quiet and a difficult target in the snowy misty air, and having a closer look. He agreed to this and I slipped away past Frank Saxby's troop who were guarding the east flank of Hingen, and drove cautiously towards the farm. I had an extraordinary view of St Joost from this angle and dimly in the foggy air could see, and of course hear, the noise of the battle going on there. It sounded and looked terrifying – flames, smoke, continuous machine-gun and rifle fire, the crack of tank guns and the whistle and crump of artillery shells which were landing towards the rear of the village. I was glad to be on my own in relative peace.

I spotted Richard's two tanks out to my left; they looked, as was so often the case, undamaged and might well have confused an enemy new to this part of the battlefield. I decided not to approach them and went on towards the farm buildings where I found no evidence of the enemy. The Firefly was still sitting nose down in the cellar. I reported this to squadron HQ and suggested that recovery of the vehicle was a practical possibility. I was curious by this time as to the whereabouts of the enemy, and decided to continue slowly along the edge of the plantation, which ran

away towards the north-east some 300 yards from the farm buildings. I saw and heard nothing from there, so continued cautiously along the side of the wood. I was within a mile of the track which ran from St Joost to Monfort when, above the noise of the battle which seemed to be easing in St Joost, I heard the clatter of tank tracks. I pulled into the wood but could see nothing; I concluded that it was the enemy retreating from St Joost and reported that to John, who ordered me to return at once. It was nearly dark by this time, the snow was falling in big soft flakes and the atmosphere was heavy with cold.

I arrived back to find that the squadron had set up a temporary mess in a building in Schilberg. I was frozen to the marrow, sick with cold and with the old pain starting in my stomach which usually presaged the return of my illness. Shortly after I had sat down, in walked Frank Hone, the padre, and John Heycock, the regimental doctor. They both cornered me and talked to me for a long time, meanwhile giving me a mug of issue rum to drink. I learned the next day that I had drunk nearly half a pint. I don't remember them leaving, but I awoke at about midday the following day after a very heavy night's sleep. I was told that Bill Pritchard had been sent back to base for a good rest, and I found out much later that Tony Hind had suggested this meeting to Frank and John as he thought that I was getting a bit 'bomb happy' and as such, could be a danger both to the squadron and myself. Bomb happy in the sense that I had started to have that feeling of invulnerability which, if exercised, could well jeopardise the lives of those under one's command. Richard Dill was in the mess with us that day and drew a cartoon of me.

Next day, St Joost having fallen, a team went out with recovery vehicles and having recovered the two damaged tanks, extricated the Firefly from the cellar. It taxed Bill Best's ingenuity as it had to be hoisted out, the tracks

Richard Dill's cartoon.

resting as they were on the rubble at the bottom of the cellar. It was a clear and sunny day and I went out to watch and then, following my route of the previous evening, drove along the track to the side of St Joost itself. It was still a smouldering ruin and I marvelled that there had been any survivors. I returned across the fields and had the extraordinary experience of following the tracks of the three German SPs which had knocked out our tanks. The tracks were crystal clear under the fresh snow and I found the shell cases which were in the field at the point from which they had fired. They were 75mm, so they were probably Mark 4 SPs. There was no cover from hedges or banks there at all and they must have been using the fog to stalk our tanks. I wondered if their engines were quieter than ours, as I didn't hear movement either before or after they had fired.

We remained in Schilberg for a few days. During this period, to my acute dismay, Colonel Cuthie left us and Desmond FitzPatrick, a Royal Hussar, was appointed as commanding officer. We all had total confidence in our old colonel and we were delighted when we heard that he had been awarded an immediate DSO for his courage and firm handling of the recent battle, but we hated the idea of losing him. Colonel Desmond came to us with a good reputation, and was accepted by us with an open mind. He had all the support that we could offer, but had yet to earn our confidence through battle.

There were several moves during the next few days, the regiment edging eastwards towards the German border. B Squadron had the privilege of being the first to cross into Germany at Waldfeucht. I was told in confidence that as part of the reorganisation, I would be leaving my beloved A Squadron and going to join Tim Pierson in the recce troop. Eventually, we returned to billets in Grevenbicht near Maesyeck. As we were settling in, Tony Case came round and told me to collect a 15cwt truck and proceed to Weert with SQMS Winch and Sgt Taylor for an investiture. Weert was about 15 miles away, on the road to Eindhoven.

We arrived at Weert at about 10 o'clock on 5 March and we were ushered into a small theatre. At 11 o'clock precisely, Field-Marshal Montgomery arrived and, after a short address, we were called on to the stage one by one; he congratulated us and pinned the decorations on to our battledresses. He spoke to everyone and in my case specifically mentioned the role that the regiment had played in the battle of St Joost. I was very impressed. He ensured that each one of us was photographed as the ceremony took place and later posed with us for a group photograph. I thought that was the end of it, but was delighted some months later to receive signed copies of both photographs. It seemed remarkable to me that a man who was so heavily engaged in a major campaign could still find time to deal with such mundane matters. I am sure that it meant a lot to all the recipients and it certainly had an effect on me. I have never forgotten the lesson that small courtesies of this nature are very important, and have tried to put that into effect throughout my life.

During the afternoon of 7 March, I was changing my clothes in my billet when Bob Ames walked along looking very grim. I made some facetious remark and then saw that he was holding out a signal for me to read. I imagined that it was my posting but before I read it he said very gently, 'Sit down and listen to me', and then, 'Your mother was killed in London yesterday in a bombing raid.' I suppose, looking back on it, I was very strung up at the time and Tony, the padre and the doctor were probably right in their diagnosis. However, on receiving this news, I was totally overwhelmed with grief and with the feeling of desolation that accompanied it. Perhaps I had never valued my mother as much as at that moment of realisation that I would never see her again. All my shortcomings in my attitude to her and my relationship with her poured into my mind, I was consumed with misery and with my feeling of guilt.

Everyone in the squadron was very kind and understanding. Colonel Desmond sent for me, gave me the use of his jeep to get to Brussels and told me to try to get back to England for the funeral and then take some leave. After considerable difficulty, helped in the end by a wandering MP who pledged his place on the plane if there was no room for me, I was flown back to Hendon, landing at lunchtime on 9 March.

I reached my grandmother's house at Chiswick and

arrived there just as the funeral party returned from the cemetery. They told me of the circumstances of her death. She had been killed by the first of the V2 rockets to land in London. It had fallen directly on her offices at Smithfield Market. She had been dead when they pulled her out of the rubble. Her rings and other jewellery had been stolen. I was consumed with hate for the Germans who had caused her death and for the thief who robbed dead bodies. My father, ever solicitous, seeing that I was unwell and angry, suggested that I should get out of London and report to an MO near his home in Winchfield; I told him that I would rather go to Bognor, where Audrey was a volunteer nurse at the Chichester Hospital. We telephoned her family, who were happy for me to go and I went down on the Sunday. I had been feeling the onset of a jaundice attack during the previous week, and on arrival in Bognor was admitted to the hospital at once. The usual blinding headaches, painful stomach and inability to retain food. Poor Audrey.

After a few days, feeling much better, I attempted to discharge myself but a steamy interview with the colonel commanding the hospital convinced me that, if I left, I would have a further medical black mark against me such as I had collected in Egypt for skipping out of the hospital in Algiers. This would affect any possibility of pension should the trouble continue to be recurrent and, as I hoped to become a regular officer, this would have been very short-sighted.

I was discharged on 5 April. Audrey and I had become engaged while I was there and I spent my last weekend with her family, before returning to London to say goodbye to my grandmother on 8 April.

I reported to the RTO on Waterloo station and, after a lot of telephoning, managed to get a berth on a ship sailing to Antwerp from the London docks. In Antwerp I went straight to the RASC and hitched a lift on a supplies convoy to Venlo, a central distribution point in north-east Holland. It was relatively easy from then on, as all trucks went east into Germany. In fact it was a salutary journey. The moment one crossed the Rhine, everywhere was in ruins, everything drab and dusty. Everywhere sullen people slinking about with averted faces; only the children, who quickly got the measure of English soldiers, were happy as they ate the issue chocolate.

I crossed the Rhine via the Xanten Bridge, which was a miracle of the Royal Engineers' skill. I had not realised how wide an obstacle the Rhine was until that moment. We then continued up the divisional centre line through Borkum to Rheine and I spent my first night at a staging post near to Osnabruck. The town had been flattened by bombing and provided the worst large-scale devastation that I had seen, although of course it was insignificant to that which we saw later. I was stunned by the totality of it and, despite my anger, horrified at the suffering which it had brought in its wake. Whatever the German people had done, I couldn't gloat over their anguish, or get satisfaction from a feeling of revenge, and already the healing process of 'selective' as opposed to 'corporate' guilt was at work in my being.

Next day, 18 April, we rattled over the bridge at Rethem, bypassed Soltau, which was still burning, and having reported my arrival to the divisional reinforcement holding unit, I went on with other reinforcements to join the regimental echelon, which had been established in some fields on the edge of woods south of Heber. I was welcomed by Titch Kirkham, who reported my arrival to the adjutant over the wireless. I spent the evening catching up on all the news, especially the casualties. The balance of my old troop were intact, but my good friend Richard Anstey was dead, blown up on a concealed 250lb bomb. He had spoken to me of his premonition of death while we were at Maeseyck and I had told him not to be so pessimistic.

Despite the sadness, everything was secondary to the general air of excitement and expectation caused by this mad rush through Germany, with the end of the war well in sight. I told Titch of my shock at the suffering among the women and children and he, in his usual blunt way, told me not to waste sympathy on the bastards. He then told me about the POW camp liberated by the regiment at Fallingborstel, and the horror of Belsen which he had visited. He then talked about the starving, mad Russian slave workers who had escaped from camps and were bent on an orgy of destruction. Apparently they were not only murderous but also cannibalistic, and orders were that if we were endangered by them and could not restrain them, then we were to shoot them. It brought my thinking back into perspective.

That evening I received orders to report to RHQ 'soonest best'. I was not to return to A Squadron but would join Tim Pierson, an ex-Northamptonshire Yeoman, as second in command of the recce troop. It was an exciting prospect, as I not only liked him very much, but also because since he had taken over the recce troop, he had gained a great reputation for initiative and courage. Most of the soldiers in it were middle Europeans, White Russians, Roumanians, and Hungarians etc., all of whom had good reason to hate the Germans and all of whom were very tough indeed. In addition to them, the troop contained a number of musicians from the regimental band. The troop was equipped with the American Chaffee tanks, Honeys, Jalopys and scout-cars, and operating as it did on the outer edge of the regiment as its eyes and ears, it was very much to my taste.

Early next morning Titch and I set off in his jeep to rendezvous with the regiment near to Welle, some 10–15 miles south of Harburg. They were carrying out sweeps in the forest, as a Hungarian SS and tank hunter group had been reported in the area. We drove in bright sunshine in an open jeep, wearing our green and gold side hats, relaxed and warmed by the sun, but although it all felt like a school picnic, somehow the quiet was ominous. Eventually, both of us shared a sense of unease, and, having not seen a soul anywhere, we stopped and checked the map. After a brief discussion, we then decided to drive on for a further two miles and if we saw nothing, to retrace our steps. Shortly afterwards we entered a dense fir forest with tall mature tree on either side and with a window of light some half a mile ahead where the road debouched from it into open country again. We saw nothing until we were about 200 yards from the exit and then our hearts missed a beat as suddenly there were tanks and men moving towards us. There was nowhere to turn and no point in running so we decided to brazen it out. Happily it turned out to be RHQ of 8th Hussars and the recce troop. They were about to carry out a regimental sweep through the very woods that we had just traversed.

Colonel Desmond was the first man to greet us. It was clear that he didn't know whether to be very angry or very amused. He compromised, welcomed me back, but told us both to be damned careful and not to become careless just because the end of the war was in sight. He then continued with the sweep. Tony Case, the adjutant, told me to find Tim Pierson who was nearby. Tim welcomed me and quickly introduced me to the members of my new troop. I was allocated a Chaffee tank, 'Hemlock III', as my command tank, plus a Humber scout-car, 'Hurstwood'. I was of course used to the latter, but the Chaffee was new to me and I became more and more impressed by its speed and manoeuvrability as the days passed. My sergeant, 'Cam' Griffiths, was excellent and we soon became good friends, while the crews were exceptional, good humoured and very willing to get on with the job whatever it might be. I felt at home immediately and experienced no feeling of strangeness.

ELEVEN

Hamburg, Hostilities End

Tim suggested that I spend the remainder of the day getting to know my troop and its equipment. We spent the night in a wood to the south of Elstorf, there was sporadic firing nearby and rumour of German troops in our immediate vicinity. I was refreshed by my leave and gladly took my turn on guard duty. I spent the first part of it in the turret using the new infra-red gunsight, which enabled one to see in the dark with remarkable clarity. Old habits prevailed, however, and I soon had to sit outside and use my own eyes and ears. Tim discussed the next day's orders with Robin Anstey – Richard's younger brother – and me. We had been allotted a flexible role protecting the flanks of the main operation, which was directed on the capture of Daerstorf and Fischbek. We were to link up with the attack being mounted to our left.

It was a misty early start as we nosed our way slowly into the wooded area between Elstorf and Vahrendorf. No opposition appeared, although we could hear via our wireless that B Squadron were already heavily engaged around Daerstorf, to our north. I could hear tanks operating very close to us, and there was obviously a battle going on in the area of Harburg. We had been briefed on this and knew that part of the division's objective was to clear the south bank of the Elbe. At about 1000hrs, we heard unidentified tanks approaching our position so we took cover. Then three Cromwells suddenly burst through the tree line and I was delighted to meet up with my old friend in the 5th Dragoon Guards, 'The Skins', Peter Duckworth. He was more surprised than I was, as none of his crews saw us until they were about 50 yards away. It gave me great confidence in the low lines of the Chaffee and its ability to be concealed. This contact having been made, we were directed north-west again but were ordered to maintain contact with the Skins' tanks.

Shortly after this, I heard the news that Wally Ryde had been killed. He was one of the most popular as well as the bravest of all the troop leaders. Tim was shattered, as he and Wally were very good friends, both having come to the regiment from the Northamptonshire Yeomanry in July 1944. Immediately after this I was told that Geoffrey Gould, who was one of my closest friends, had been seriously wounded in the head. It all seemed so tragic with the end of the war seemingly in sight, but the major effect on me was to make me want to do something positive rather than cruise about as an armoured liaison officer. I was delighted when we were ordered to proceed to Daerstorf and take up watching positions overlooking the Elbe.

It was my first view of that river and we could see for miles across the flat, wooded and peaceful-looking plain through which it flowed. We stayed in the same area, firstly with C Squadron and then A Squadron for some days, always in a watching role. Below us was the village of Fischbek where there was a Belgian prisoner-of-war camp, full of sick and mainly elderly officers. These were liberated, the fitter of them were evacuated, and I was able to practise my French again.

Occasionally we were involved in the movement of any German prisoners who appeared. I recall one such incident very clearly, when a German major and about ten German soldiers surrendered. He was without doubt the most pompous German that I have ever encountered, and, quoting the Geneva Convention, refused to ride on the back of my tank with 'other ranks'. Bob Butterfield, then Sargeant-Major of A Squadron, was nearby at the time, and before I could do anything he said, 'All right, sir. I'll arrange for him to go back alone with my tank,' and ushered him away. It was about two miles back to the collection point and when I got there, there was no sign of the major. I became somewhat anxious that Bob had taken the law into his own hands as all ranks were very uptight after the death of Wally. However, about ten minutes later a Cromwell tank roared up, with the usual clouds of dust and smoke. Trotting along behind it was the man himself, thick with dust and sweat; he had travelled alone as requested. He was speechless and although I couldn't approve officially, I must confess to a certain satisfaction. I hope that it was a lesson to him.

We became experts on the layout of villages and hamlets between Buxtehude and Harburg, and from time to time experienced alarms and stand-tos as a result of enemy movements. Apart from this, there was the elation of knowing that it was all very nearly over, and we enjoyed the hot summer days.

Saturday 28 April is still ingrained in my memory, as it was a day during which I came as close to death as I had ever been, but this time from 'friendly fire'. We were on the high ground overlooking Fischbek village, where we had identified a barracks in which there were more Belgian prisoners of war. I had gone forward some 100 yards to obtain a better vantage point and to show one of B Squadron officers the layout of the building. 'Luger' Much, my gunner, was in the turret of my tank giving us cover. It was a baking hot day, all was quiet and the world seemed at peace. We finished our reconnaissance, returned to the front of my tank and stood there for a minute chatting, my head directly in line with the muzzle of the main gun. Suddenly

The Chaffee, 'Hemlock III'.

there was a great burst of machine-gun fire which whipped around us and we both threw ourselves to the ground. Then the silence, until the red face of Much appeared at the top of the turret. I was not at all mollified when he explained that he had dozed off and trodden on the firing button. The Browning 300 machine-gun was mounted co-axially with the main armament, so the burst could not have missed me by more than a couple of inches.

That night, we sent a party down to Fischbek to liberate the Belgians but it was felt that they were better left there for the time being. I met some of them, including Henri du Page, whom I saw frequently in Brussels afterwards and Albert Libion, later brigadier in the Premières Guides. The latter was a most amusing fellow. His daughter had been born while he was a prisoner, on the day that the British captured Derna in North Africa. He had named her Derna after the victory – poor girl! (Albert rejoined his regiment and when, in 1947, I was on the staff of 7th Armoured Brigade, he was stationed at Soest and we met very often.)

Next morning, Sunday, we heard Mass in the field just behind my tanks and afterwards the padre came back with me to have a cup of tea. While drinking it, we idly looked out over the valley below us. I was pointing out to him the red brick buildings which had housed the Belgians, when suddenly a German Kubelwagen appeared bearing a large white flag. It proceeded very slowly and hesitantly up the hill and crossing our front, covered by our guns, reached the road at a track junction about 200 yards to our right. We had notified B Squadron, and I was a member of the reception committee waiting as they arrived at the top of the hill. The vehicle contained a driver and two officers. I said 'Guten tag' to the older of the two officers, who said something in reply but my schoolboy German was inadequate. They were all whisked away, then blindfolded I believe, and taken to divisional HQ.

In 1963 I was in Hamburg and mentioned this incident to a German friend of mine. I then received a letter from General Konsul Dr G.A. Link which reads:

General Konsul Dr G. A. Link
Hamburg
7 May 1963

Dear Major Bellamy

Mr Kruger conveyed greetings of you to me these days.

I was glad to hear from you again and think that it is a funny coincidence that through Mr Kruger and the Opera House we get in contact again. I very well remember you and the events around the beginning of May 1945. So it would be very nice if you come and see me one day in Hamburg, and we shall have a long talk on those exciting hours which we spent together.

Some years ago I have met your former comrade Lindsey of the 7th Armoured Division occasionally. I also hear from Bill Mather Lt Colonel the 1st British officer to cross the Elbe bridges on 3rd May 1945 . . .

We met, subsequently, in the Hamburg Opera House. He had identified me by recalling the green and gold side hat which I should not have been wearing! He stressed how courteously they had been treated and how great an effect this had had on the way that they reported back to the higher command. He also said how worried they had been as they emerged into the open, knowing that we were there with tanks and not knowing if we would respect the white flag. He added that if they had been on the Russian front they would have been shot.

During the following few days we heard the report of Hitler's suicide in Berlin, learned of the rapid advances on all fronts by the Allies, and the strong rumours that Hamburg was about to surrender. On 3 May we stood by to move into Hamburg, which had indeed surrendered. Our entry was delayed and in fact we drove over the Elbe Bridge during the early hours of 4 May. Hamburg was a most horrifying and astonishing sight, for which all the newspaper articles and previous experiences in the war, including bombed London, had been unable to prepare us. The approach to the bridge showed to some degree the damage which had been inflicted, but as we emerged from the metal confines of the bridge itself, the full magnitude of the devastation could be appreciated. Hamburg had been destroyed. Roads were nothing but gaps in the mountains of rubble. To our left and right were huge concrete air-raid shelters surrounded by a wasteland in which stood battered buildings.

On our right-hand side, as we entered the dockland area, were rows of houses which at first sight appeared to be intact, but I then realised, with horror, that they were mere burnt-out shells. The horizontal black and reddish streaks across the face of buildings were caused by the hundred-mile-per-hour furnace-like winds that the fire bombing had been designed to cause. There would have been little chance of escape for young or old. The whole place stank of death.

Initially my return to Germany after my mother's death had been coloured by my desire for vengeance. I wanted to hate the German race – full stop. Osnabruck muted this feeling and I started to experience true compassion for the elderly, the women and the children, but it was the sight of the devastation in Hamburg that finally brought me to my senses. We knew the triumph of victory and of killing the enemy force so as to advance our own cause. Now I was seeing, in full measure, the agony of non-combatant death on a large scale and the consequent anguish that it brought to the whole society. I felt very uncomfortable about it all.

The docks themselves too, were an extraordinary sight. I was ordered to halt there for about twenty minutes, blocking off a side road while the remainder of the regiment passed through. I have never seen such a mass of con torted metal as those huge cranes and gantries, deformed by heat and blast into the most inconceivable shapes. Knotted girders, blackened or reddened, some drooping where enormous heat had melted the steel; it was an unforgettable scene. One could hardly tell the water from the land, as so many of the structures were lying in the docks themselves.

As we penetrated still further I saw the fuselage of a Lancaster bomber lying on top of one of the air raid shelters, where it had evidently crashed some months before. There were few people about and we were told later that most of the city slept in the suburbs or had been evacuated to the country due to the bombing.

We were travelling with regimental HQ and were directed to disperse when we reached the Alte-See, the lake in the centre of the city. Our first call was to the eastern side of the lake, but, as we arrived, Richard Dill was being evicted from the Atlantic Hotel by the headquarters staff of 53rd Welsh Division who had been allocated it as their HQ. He was greatly displeased as he and Pat de Clermont had just organised a champagne breakfast to be served by the hotel manager. We returned to the southern end of the lake, since the central bridge was unsafe, and went up past the Vier Jahrezeiten Hotel, later the Officers' Club, to a small boat house and garden opposite the gauleiter's residence. RHQ were already installed there. It was a bright day and the sun was warming up as we cooked breakfast, watched by one or two German civilians and the inevitable clutch of hungry children. The non-fraternisation ban had been announced, and we were at a loss as to how to handle the consequent problem. It is not within the mentality of the average British soldier to bear grudges, to ignore pretty girls, and to fail to show affection to children. However we kept stern faces and maintained our lofty pose of indifference by walking past them without acknowledging their presence in any way. Actually those of the troop who were Middle-European or German did not at this stage find that too difficult.

Breakfast finished, we wandered over to the gauleiter's house. It was undamaged as far as I could see. The splendid entrance was marbled, very ornate, and had contained a lot of flags and other decorations which had been taken off the walls. We were not allowed upstairs but went down a small marble staircase to the lower floor. On the right-hand side was a room about 30 feet long and 15 to 20 feet wide, again marbled throughout. This contained a sort of altar at one end and various devices which were clearly representing the masonry of Hitlerism and the SS. There were daggers, swastikas in various forms and books and memorabilia, all of which were facets of the almost religious ceremonies which must have taken place there. In the centre was a fine bust of the late Führer himself, with a cigarette stuck in his mouth! The whole place felt sacrilegious to me and I was glad to escape into the fresh air. On one of the benches I found a Nazi swastika armband, which I kept.

Meanwhile, however, my troop had discovered some band instruments in the basement of the house and as I emerged,

I was greeted with loud, harmonious 'oompa music'. They were grouped around one of the corporals in the regimental band, some dressed in Nazi hats or bits of Nazi uniform, all playing their hearts out in the morning sunshine. It was a scene of great humour and made us all feel much better. This went on with my enthusiastic support for about a quarter of an hour, while German civilians watched us somewhat nervously. I then noticed a staff-car driving along the road with both General Lyne, our divisional commander and Colonel Desmond in it. They did not look pleased. I was sent for, given an imperial rocket, told to return the instruments and together with the troop dispatched to watch the northern approaches to the city.

It was about 1130hrs by this time and the sun was blazing down on us as we made our way through the rubble, trying to find the Pinnenburg road. We passed by B Squadron, who were guarding what was left of the railway station, and then went out into uncharted country. There were mountains of rubble on either side of us with German civilians appearing out of holes, presumably their cellars etc., while lines of dusty, dispirited German soldiers trudged down the road. Most of them were in unguarded columns as they had already been disarmed. We also passed horse drawn vehicles, one of which, with metal barrels on it, was the local water supply for the neighbourhood, and anxious housewives were out with containers, presumably collecting their day's ration.

As we progressed further into the suburbs, so the damage lessened, although it was very deceptive, as often the front of a building seemed to be undamaged while in fact there was nothing standing behind it. We formed road blocks, disarming the Germans as they came in. There was little excitement, but on one occasion I saw a crowd of soldiers gathering around a batch of prisoners, so I went over to see what the trouble was. I was horrified to find that they were clamouring for the autograph of a particularly large and dirty German. It was Max Schmelling, the famous heavyweight boxer of pre-war days. This was 'fraternisation' so I sent him on his way, to the annoyance of those who hadn't yet obtained his autograph. That evening we were sent into a concentration area north of Hamburg, and the news broke that the ceasefire was to take effect in three days' time. There was little sense of victory and no exuberance among us. It seemed odd to have to wait a further three days and although relieved, we weren't able to really grasp the truth of it until it became a fait accompli.

After the weekend we heard that VE Day was to be at 0001hrs on Wednesday 9 May, and that we were to move north towards Kiel. The SS troops were to lay down their arms on the east side of the Schleswig-Holstein peninsula, and our role was to prevent them from making their escape back into the community. As we moved north so we visited certain houses, the homes of known Nazis or SS officers. I went to one of them with my troop. It was a nice modern house with a charming and well-kept garden. There was nobody at home but everywhere photographs of the officer himself and his wife and family. In the garage was an 8-cylinder Mercedes Benz coupé which it seemed a pity to leave, and Tony Hind was persuaded, without much difficulty, to drive it north with the regiment. Unfortunately it was appropriated together with other vehicles of similar quality when an amnesty for handing in such 'spoils of war' was declared shortly after VE Day. Not, however, before we had driven it at high speed along one of the undamaged sections of the autobahn between Bremen and Hamburg.

We reached Wachen that evening and, having searched the place for SS troops, settled down for the night in the knowledge that the next day it would be all over. I was especially fortunate that day to wander into a nearby barn and discover a German paratrooper's motorcycle. It gave us immense pleasure as we took in turns to roar up and down an impromptu obstacle course.

On Sunday 6 May there was a very moving church service taken by our padre, Frank Hone. It was standard in all units and ended with a mighty singing of 'Now thank we all our God'. Very satisfying. Later, the colonel visited us. After a few drinks, he rode the motorcycle with great skill and I took a photograph of him in action. We were all very impressed. VE Day itself seemed almost an anti-climax, and only rated ten lines in regimental orders.

Although I believe many members of the regiment got together and celebrated VE night with a bonfire, showers of Very lights and singing, we in recce troop didn't seem to react that way. We had a good meal, a few drinks and then separated into small groups of rather pensive men talking and wondering about the future. I remember sitting with two members of the troop, one White Russian and one Hungarian, both Jewish, both still very bitter and both worried as to their future. I was too young to really understand it all, but it did bring home to me the difficulties facing those who were displaced by the war. The termination of hostilities meant to many of them the beginning of the survival struggle and not the end of it.

On 10 May, we went to Schwabstedt, where I was delighted to find myself attached to A Squadron again. I really enjoyed our stay there. It was a very small village on the edge of a large mere, marshy and very peaceful. The inhabitants, still very apprehensive, did not intrude on our existence and we set up our various messes in barns or commandeered farm buildings and enjoyed the chance of settling in one place for a little while. Nearby was a splendid example of the old wooden German windmill and I spent many hours there entranced by the noise, the all-pervading dust and the furious shaking movements. It stood about 50 feet high and was pivoted on a single central post. The miller cranked it round so as to catch the wind in its latticed sails, which rotated at an alarming rate in the strong winds of that area. Inside there was tremendous vibration, the whoosh as the sails flew past the small vision slits, and all the time the rumble of the grinding mechanism and the clouds of flour everywhere. The miller was a fat, jovial, drunken giant. He made me welcome from the start, and despite the 'non-frat' ban I had no difficulty in enjoying his presence at the mill itself. I did not, however, accept his invitations to the house.

We took our turn as guards on the roads from the coast where the SS were held, and monitored the traffic very carefully. In Schwabstedt itself we still saw thousands of unarmed German soldiers making their way south. They were either on foot or they were riding in horse-drawn transport. There were also thousands of displaced persons, all trying to make their way back to their homeland. Some were from Poland and many from East Germany, Silesia, Latvia, Estonia and Lithuania. All were totally bewildered as to what to do, as they had been evicted by our allies the Russians in the first place. Later I developed a deep personal interest in the displaced persons problem and for some time worked alongside the Catholic relief team (CCRA) based at Greven near Munster.

I remember well one rather dumpy little girl of about 16 years old, who came to me while we were in Schwabstedt. She was East German, had been a refugee from the Russian invasion and had attached herself as 'comforter' to a German tank crew as they retreated. In return for her services, they fed her and they brought her back with them but now, prisoners themselves, they had abandoned her. She offered herself to me for all purposes, provided that I would feed her and give her shelter. She had nothing except a blanket and the clothes she stood up in. She believed that her parents had been killed, knew that her home was now in the Russian Zone and had no contacts this side of the Oder. We kitted her out with some food and an old haversack and sent her on down the road saying that there was help to be had in Hamburg. I only hope that she found some kindly folk who would protect her. There must have been tens of thousands of similar cases.

We saw little of the SS at our road blocks and I was astonished one day when a very clean and smart German Kügelwagen appeared. It was driven by an SS soldier and, by his side, on a stretcher was a very badly wounded SS officer. 'Luger' Much, my driver, was with me at the time and he searched the vehicle while I stood watching. The officer was obviously in considerable pain; he was a ghastly colour and seemed to be close to death. Much lifted his blankets gently and disclosed bandages and gore from his chest downwards. 'Mochten-sie ein cigarette,' I said, it all seemed too horrible. 'My dear fellow,' he whispered, 'nothing would be nicer.' I was rather taken aback. His English was perfect. I lit a cigarette and put it between his lips, to Much's evident disapproval. He told me that he had been up at Oxford before the war studying Classics. As they left, he lifted one hand from under the blankets and handed me a camera, which I refused, so he gave it to Much saying, 'If your bloody second line troops are anything like ours, I shall soon be robbed of this and I would rather see it go to a fighting soldier.' I let them through under escort to go straight to the RAP (regimental aid post), and he was seen by the Regimental Medical Officer before going on to another hospital. The jeep and the SS soldier returned later. I purchased the camera from Much for £5; it was a Zeiss Super Ikonta, and I took some excellent pictures with it during the next five years in Germany.

Tim Pierson had been sent on leave at the end of the war, so I was enjoying the command of the recce troop. I had obtained a Union Jack somewhere along the line and this flew proudly at my troop HQ. We were visited there by General Lyne, who expressed himself as pleased with our set-up. There was a marvellous moment when, at the end of the inspection of A Squadron, the general asked the squadron leader if there was anything else to see. He turned to the sergeant major who, standing stiffly to attention, replied, 'The general hasn't seen our shit'ouses, sumps and latrines, SAH.' The general complied without demur.

We left Schwabstedt for Agethorst, near Itzehoe, and took up residence in a very attractive old farm and its surrounding cottages. We considered our troop billets to be quite luxurious, although they lacked such basic facilities as running water. We were told that we could be in Agethorst for three months, so the regiment began to assemble a stableful of horses. Many came from the army veterinary centre in Delmenhorst, and there was a constant stream of 8th Hussar officers with 3-ton trucks visiting there, selecting potentially good mounts and bringing them back to our stables. My riding experience had been confined to Suffolk Punches at Cranford before the war, so I was content to accept other people's recommendation. Eventually I was allocated a quiet, comfortable chestnut called Dante, with a beautiful roman nose. Dante and I got on well together and I rode happily every day, watched by eagle-eyed experts such as Major 'Punch' Dunne.

The washing facilities were so bad that we used the stable pump as shower; one pumping, the other washing. There were three attractive German girls in the village who seemed to make it their business to be around the yard as this ceremony took place. We, insofar as it was possible when shuddering with the cold shower and being stark naked, adopted a pose of lofty indifference. One of these girls was overheard to say that frat or non-frat she would bed an English officer before they left Agethorst!

A member of my troop told me the story of a kind-hearted Polish girl, a foreign worker, who had been brought from Poland to Germany to work on the farms. Being Polish, she was not in 'purdah' and took her place in the social life of the camp. She was not averse to sleeping with the soldiery. Apparently, her bed was under the window in one of the outhouses, and one night this chap was in bed with her, and, he said, 'doing his duty!' when a head popped through the window and a hand started running up and down the back of his legs. It was, he said, pitch dark and he lay there paralysed, recognising the voice as that of a senior NCO, who was, 'murmuring words of tender endearment at the same time'. He admitted that his one fear was that this NCO would run his hand down low enough to discover that the legs which he was fondling ended in a pair of army boots! Luckily the voice receded and the danger passed. 'Stopped my gallop though,' he said.

At the beginning of June, we held the first horse show in the Rhine Army, which was attended by the corps commander, General Barker. It was a great success and some sixty entrants enjoyed competing over a very professional course. Richard Dill imported the first elements of the regimental beagle pack, the Royal Navy cooperating in their transportation to Germany. We held a number of paperchases and at the same time managed to carry out our not very onerous duties as far as policing was concerned. There were moments of activity such as those when we undertook searches for escaped senior Nazis who were reported in the area, but little else. The German singer who had made the song 'Lili Marlene' so well known came in person to 'Shepherd's', the 7th Armoured Divisional officers' club in Itzehoe. I went and heard her sing that famous song, which was almost the signature tune of the division. She looked to me to be very apprehensive, a not-so-young woman, who had come to the club under some duress. However, surrounded by the evident goodwill of all those present, she relaxed during the evening and everyone joined in the singing with gusto.

About the middle of June a rumour spread around the regiment that we were to go to Berlin. About the same time a load of battleship grey paint appeared by courtesy of the German naval stores, Lübeck. This was to help us to clean up the tanks, and added further fuel to that rumour. Nobody was surprised when eventually the official word came that the division was to proceed there on wheels or tank-transporters during the first week in July, and there was general delight when it was announced that we would take part in the Victory Parade which was to be held there later in the month.

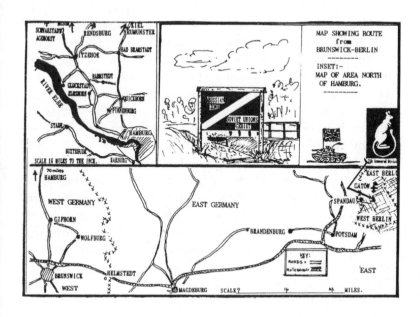

TWELVE

Recce Troop,
HQ Squadron, Berlin

On 4 July, we loaded the tanks on to their transporters for the long journey down to the marshalling area which was to be Gifhorn, a village slightly to the north of Brunswick. I was lucky enough to drive there in my Humber scout-car, 'Hurstwood', so although we were in the regimental convoy which followed the autobahn, I was able to slip away from time to time and have a general look at the countryside. Once south of Hamburg it became very flat, uninteresting heathland with woods and a few villages. This was to become one of our main tank and artillery training areas later. There was little evidence of war, although I did see one small airfield where the wreckage of several planes lay destroyed on the ground.

That evening, we offloaded the tanks and went into leaguer. Herbert Firth, who was commanding the contingent during this phase of the move, told us that we were to proceed to Berlin on our own tracks, a journey of about 125 miles. We were enthusiastic about going to Berlin, but to most of us it appeared to be more like a journey into enemy territory than a meeting with friends. The fact that by going on tracks the regiment retained a measure of its war footing seemed to bear this out.

One of the exceptions to this ambivalent feeling was Sgt Howard, a recent promotion which he richly deserved, who was telling us all what a pleasure it would be to meet our Russian allies. He was, I knew, a dedicated communist/ socialist whose uncle had fought in the International Brigade during the Spanish war. Personally, I was too politically immature to feel strongly one way or the other. As a Catholic, I found the creed of communism unacceptable, but equally I was aware of my responsibilities for caring for my neighbour and after months of exposure to the persuasive Alan, I was beginning to feel that socialist principles were more in keeping with my ideals. It didn't weigh very heavily on my mind. The excitement of the journey, and the fact that we were to visit so famous a destination, was enough to blot out any 'political' worries that I might have had.

Herbert excelled himself during the two days that we were there. He was determined to ensure that the regiment's tanks were immaculate, and it was he, I believe, who had originally located the hoard of grey paint with which we had repainted every armoured vehicle while we were in Agethorst. In Brunswick, however, he found a top-coat varnish which in his view enhanced the finish, and he proceeded to paint his own squadron of tanks with this. This changed the colour effect, was unable to be removed, and so in some haste the whole regiment had to follow suit. Not a very popular officer at the time!

Early on Saturday 7 July, we set off for Berlin; it was a warm and lovely summer morning. It promised to be a significant journey for us all, but most especially for those who had served with the regiment from the bleakest days in North Africa, when our chances of ultimate victory had looked slim. Our convoy travelled at a steady 20–30 mph on an autobahn, the surface of which was a little damaged. We saw Russian soldiers on guard near the frontier, which was unguarded on our side and marked only by a simple wooden sign. There was a long delay at one point, while papers were cleared and permission obtained from some source higher up the chain for us to proceed. Most of the bridges were destroyed, causing further delays as we had to make detours. On each occasion there were Russian soldiers guarding the route. It was noticeable that, even at this stage, there was no real attempt to fraternise by either side. No waving or shouting and certainly at the front of the convoy, where I was with the reece troop and RHQ, I saw no exchanges of any sort. It struck me quite forcibly at the time, as we were used to seeing at least cigarettes and food exchanged or offered; I found it all rather chilling.

Approaching the outskirts of Berlin there was little immediate evidence of the battle. Vision was restricted as it was flattish, wooded country and the autobahn had high banks in many places, so one didn't get the same grandstand view that we experienced on entering Hamburg. Then suddenly we debouched from the autobahn on to streets where virtually everything had been damaged or destroyed. Mounds of rubble, tottering walls, blocked side streets, a sense of total dereliction, and among this devastation, children, young and elderly women and a few old men. Everything seemed drab and dirty. My first impressions were that it was similar to the bomb havoc which we had seen in Hamburg.

By this time it was about 2000hrs and as we swung in towards the Adolf-Hitler Platz, we saw our brigadier, Brig Spurling, standing on the back of his scout-car which was parked at the side of the road. As we drove past he took the salute, watched by a few civilians, some of whom clapped as we went by. This made me wonder whether we were going to be considered as liberators by some of the indigenous population.

A vehicle from the advance party met us and led us to the Charlottenburg Chaussee, where we turned left down a gentle hill, damaged buildings on either side. At the point where we turned there was a German tank with its turret blown off. There were more civilians to be seen by this time and also small groups of heavily armed Russian soldiers walking about. Nobody appeared to notice us as we rumbled past. After some time, the road opened up into a wide avenue, with the 1936 Olympic Games buildings facing us at the bottom. The buildings facing us formed a semi-circle and gave the impression that they were composed of segmented colonnades. At the front and central to the edifice were two tall, solid-looking, stone pillars and flanking those were dozens of flag-poles. These stretched in a line towards us across a vast cobbled platz, the Olympischer Sportz Platz, itself divided into squares by white paving stones. It was reminiscent of the photographs of the 1936 Games that I had seen in the newspapers, as we had followed those games avidly while at school. I remember that my heroes were the British 4 2 400 yards team who gained the gold medal, and of course Jesse Owens of the USA who won four gold medals but whom Hitler ignored.

The building seemed very impressive as we drove down on to the square and lined up the vehicles by squadrons, but on closer inspection we found that it was badly damaged, looted and crammed with filth. The advance party had done a marvellous job and the billets themselves were not bad despite the surrounding debris. A meal had been prepared and it was a relief for everyone to start to settle in. The officers had been allocated quarters in adjacent houses in Charlottenburg, an area which was, relatively speaking, undamaged. These houses had been emptied of their occupants. It was not a night when we felt like exploring things, everyone was dog tired and we fell into bed and slept.

Next day was devoted to maintenance and to sprucing up the vehicles ready for the Victory Parade. At some point in the morning, I was asked to keep an eye on some of the German workers who were cleaning out the buildings. I hadn't had a chance to go into any of the rooms before and I was horrified at the disgusting way that the Russian soldiers had behaved. Looting, after all they had endured, I could understand, but the wanton destruction was appalling. Everything was torn off the walls, all sanitary fittings destroyed, drawers and cupboards were full of excrement, and it seemed as if there had been a deliberate attempt to foul the place before we arrived to take over. This was certainly the impression obtained by a lot of the troop, and attitudes towards the Russian soldiers hardened as a result. Civilian workers had been conscripted to clean the place up, but the stench was so bad they had to have a stretcher party available to carry out those who fainted. I was glad to get back to the tank park.

During that first afternoon I walked up the road towards Berlin with several members of my troop and, seeing a small public park sited there among the debris, went over to have a look at it. One of the chaps with me that day was Tpr Melnik, a White Russian, and a fluent Russian speaker, who, later, was to be used with another Russian member of the troop as an interpreter with one of the committees at the Potsdam summit. As we entered the garden, seven Russian soldiers, armed to the teeth, appeared on the other side of it, about 50 yards away. They looked villainous and very scruffy. I was uncertain as to what to do but Melnik shouted 'Hello', they waved, smiled back at us and we all walked towards the centre of the gardens. I handed round my big silver cigarette case, a present from my mother, which held thirty Woodbines, and we all exchanged nods and smiles while we lit up. My case incidentally was emptied. Meanwhile Melnik started to talk to them and to translate the substance back to us.

One of the Russian soldiers had a sack with him which he opened and which contained a variety of household items, candlesticks, photograph frames and trinkets. On enquiry he apparently said that they were available everywhere if you asked in the right way. At this point he raised his machine-gun in my direction and grinned at me. I felt a bit vulnerable with my silver cigarette case and made a mental note not to offer cigarettes in it again. The conversation then became more general and they told us that they were from a Mongolian division. We gathered that they had not been directly involved in the capture of the city but that they had been promised the chance of 'occupying it'; by the look on their faces as they said this, I saw that to them, this meant 'sacking it'. They were now engaged in doing just that. I asked them if they knew that this was the British Zone now. Among them was a rather chunky looking young man, who I then realised was an officer. He became quite aggressive and said that they didn't give a f—— whose zone it was, they had fought the war, we'd done f—— all, and they were quite ready to carry on and fight us. It was an uncomfortable moment and although Melnik handled it very well and we parted with smiles, we all agreed afterward, that we had watched our backs as we walked away.

Life settled quickly into a routine and we scrubbed and polished, kit inspections, drills, squadron inspections and finally a regimental inspection, at the end of which Pat de Clermont, who was commanding in Colonel Desmond's absence in England, expressed himself as 'reasonably satisfied'. That evening saw us enjoying a monumental party in the Officers' Mess, definitely noisy, full of fun and the drink flowed liberally. I can't actually remember going to bed, but next day I was assured that I had done so without any problems. However we were due to have a practice parade on the following morning at dawn. The first thing that I knew about it, was the blast of a jeep horn outside my billet. I looked out and all the other officers from my billet were already in place and raring to go. I dressed in 30 seconds flat, rushed downstairs ramming my pistol into its holster, leapt into the jeep and staggered into position in front of my troop just in time. Pat de Clermont walked past me on his way to the RHQ tanks which were alongside ours,

'Very original, dear boy, but is it effective?' he asked, pointing to my pistol holster. I looked down. I had holstered my ivory handled hairbrush in my mad rush!

The practice parades weren't very exciting, but they did give one a splendid view of Berlin and the extent of the devastation. We travelled the length of the Charlottenburg Chaussee, as far as the Branden-berger Tür, the great triumphal gate which now marked the divide between the British and the Russian zones. We passed the Tiergarten (Zoological Gardens), and the Siegessaule, a 210-foot column commemorating German victory in the 1870 Franco-Prussian War, complete with the gilded angel, triumphal wreath in hand, still intact on the top. You could climb up inside this column and gain the most wonderful, panoramic view of the city and its suburbs. Then there was the Reichstag and most of the old government buildings, as well as the great ruined church, the Mariankirke. I think that I was more impressed by the state of the trees in the parks on either side of the avenue than anything else. They were virtually stripped of their leaves and most of the lower branches had been ripped off them as well, making them look like the aftermath of a First World War battle. The fighting must have been horrific.

As far as the practice itself was concerned, once we had settled ourselves into the required order, we moved off in line by squadrons: RHQ first, followed by the recce troop, then A Squadron and the rest. I was in the first of the regiment's tanks in the outside line adjacent to the saluting base, so I was well placed for a good view. It also meant that I set the position of this line for the whole regiment, so it needed care. My corporal, Cpl Cohen, concentrated on keeping us in position as to the line abreast and I watched the line ahead, as we rolled at some 15mph down the immense avenue. It all worked very well.

Fired by the sights that we had seen, Bob Ames, Johnny Robertson and I went off in a jeep one afternoon to have a closer look at the centre of the city. We drove up to the Brandenburger Tür and went into the Russian Zone. There were no guards at the border between the two sectors. Later, we had strict instructions not to pass through without divisional authorisation. The signs at the gate were all in Russian and beyond and to the side of the roads was a huge poster with a picture of Stalin on it. On our left, just inside the British Zone was a Russian war memorial with a T-34 tank mounted on an oblong plinth, opposite this was a rather brash edifice with gaudy posters of Stalin, Churchill and Truman. It was not really the sort of thing that impressed any of us. By this time we were very critical of the Russian soldiers' behaviour, their discipline and their turn out. We watched the 'ceremonial' guards on duty at their war memorial and were appalled at their sloppy dress and their drill. 'Look like a lot of bloody sanitary orderlies,' remarked the mirror-booted and totally immaculate Sgt Arnold.

East Berlin was very drab, there wasn't a lot of activity and actually there were not many Russian soldiers to be seen. There appeared to be few shops open, but in every way compared with our sector it seemed very boring, so we turned round at the top of the Unter den Linden where the road splits into five major roadways, and returned to the Brandenberger Tür.

We visited the Reichstag first; this was a total burned-out ruin but we saw the tower on which the famous photograph of the Russian soldiers hoisting the national flag was taken. Then on to the Reich Chancellerei, walking up the wide ceremonial steps through the front door and into the spacious entrance hall. The building was wrecked, ripped by shellfire and showed graphically the intensity of the battle that was fought in and around it. A Russian guard was on duty at the door but he ignored us. We wandered into Hitler's study, where only an empty desk remained, drawers scattered all over the floor, a huge stucco German eagle dominating the wall behind it. Then into other huge offices, everywhere the floors were littered with papers. I picked up visiting cards from Julius Schaub, SS Gruppenfuhrer, and Georg Thierack, the Reich Minister of Justice. There were thousands of cards and documents lying about everywhere, and a historian would have given his eyes to have been there to sort through them. Eventually we looked out of a window and saw a small garden at the back where, we had been told, Hitler's bunker was sited and where the bodies of Hitler and Eve Braun were burned by his chauffeur after they had committed suicide. There was a Russian guard there who made it quite clear that it was 'off limits', swinging his gun towards us. We didn't dally!

It was an eerie building and I felt as if I had been present just after the sack of Rome by the Goths. There was something very unwholesome about it all, evil really, and the heavy humourless Russian presence didn't do much to help. It was oppressive, and instinctively each of us wanted to return to the sunshine and to life outside. As we were walking out, Bob pointed to a small room, rather like a cloakroom, just off the main hall, and we walked over casually to have a look inside. The room was equipped with long metal racks and we found that these were stacked with engravings, etchings, prints and paintings, presumably all 'presents' looted from occupied countries or 'gifts' to Hitler. We all took a few engravings as souvenirs and I still have some of them now. I picked up a handful of papers off the floor and found that they were signed by Hitler and were cards sending Christmas greetings to friends, to be enclosed with a small gift which he had received from the captured territories. I felt slightly nervous walking out with my handful of papers but the sentry seemed uninterested.

We drove to the old Kurfürstendamm, the famous shopping street, now a total shambles. There were still a few shops open and some stalls with vegetables and presumably rationed foodstuff. There were many more people about, including a number of soldiers, mainly Russian and American but some groups of British soldiers as well. It was warm, the sky was blue and despite the tragedy so evident around us, life was beginning to pick up again. I was surprised to note that some of the girls were not only pretty but also quite well dressed. Despite the non-fraternisation ban it was difficult not to look at them appreciatively and to smile occasionally. Some of the smiles were returned, we began to feel more welcome and less enthusiastic about the 'non-frat' ban. When one considered their situation, it was amazing really that there were still signs of good humour even at this early stage of the occupation.

We visited the famous Adlon Hotel, one of the social centres of Nazism. It had been turned into a fortress, and was very badly damaged, but the name sign still remained over the front door as did the two great carriage lamps outside. As we left, we saw that a crowd had gathered in a corner of the square, so, leaving in the jeep, Johnnie and I wandered over to see what was going on. As we approached we saw that standing among the Germans, were Russian, American and a few British soldiers. We stood back and watched for a minute before getting closer. It became evident that this was a 'black market' and goods were changing hands. We were not quite certain as to what action we ought to take but decided that in this case a discreet retreat was the wisest course. As we turned away one young American came past holding a Luger pistol which he showed to us very proudly. He had bought it for 100 Camel cigarettes from a Russian soldier. 'Gee, fellers, you want to get in there,' he said, 'You can get anything from women to watches for cigarettes. I'm going back for more.' With that he went.

At that time, the Reichsmark was 40 to the pound, and all old Reichsmark notes of up to 10 RM were still valid. The dollar was also currency at about 10 RM to the dollar, i.e. $4 = £1. The Deutschmark did not come in until 1948. Money was really only used by the big dealers, who dealt in truck loads, working with the professional crooks from the US base at Frankfurt or the British base in Antwerp. These were investigated by the military police team.

Most of the occupying forces were looking for souvenirs like German pistols, Lugers, cameras, watches, silver, or sex and for these they used cigarettes, not cash. These were valued at 5 RM per cigarette and the military issue at that time was 100 cigarettes per week per man, costing us 10s. So on a straight swop basis 10s became worth 500 RM or £12.10s, not a bad return when you remember that a trooper received about 28s per week. My pay as senior subaltern was £19 per month i.e. about £4.10s per week. The soldiers, by cashing in on the value of their cigarettes, brought a flood of 10 RM notes into the NAAFI and, whereas the calculated money in circulation should have been around £1,000,000, within two months it was running at over £10,000,000 as the soldiers, having changed fags for cash, then spent it on food or drink at the NAAFI. The authorities couldn't stem this, so Reichmarks went out as a currency in the British Zone and we were paid in BAFs, British Army Forces Vouchers, an occupation currency which was only valid in our NAAFI shops or clubs.

Continuing our tour, we turned down a partially blocked side road bounded by heaps of rubble, and for the first time we saw gangs of women working with shovels and buckets to clear the debris. It seemed an impossible task, but I believe that in fact they did achieve ultimate success, clearing up the city without much mechanical aid. Eventually, of course, the returning prisoners of war helped, as did the other men as they filtered back to the city.

On 12 July the regiment provided tanks for the parade at the Brandenberger Tür, during which Field Marshal Montgomery presented British decorations to Marshals

Zhukov and Rokossovsky. The tank guard of honour comprised two troops taken from each Cromwell squadron, and as the recce troop was not directly involved, I was allowed to watch the proceedings from the 'touchline'. The Russians outnumbered the British by about three to one; they were quite smart in their loosely cut service dress – although I am sure that our regimental tailors, Rogers, would have had a fit – flat hats, gold or silver epaulettes and polished jackboots. The British contingent, in striking contrast, wore simple battle dress and brown shoes. One of the things that impressed me was the towering backcloth of ruined, burnt out buildings, it was very much a 'war scene', and as such, very dramatic. All the Russians had so many medals on their chests already that I wondered where they could possibly put ours!

The pressure continued, and on the next day we held a divisional victory parade as a full dress rehearsal for the 'real' victory parade to follow. Once again we were blessed with fine weather and in due course, having been inspected by General Lyne, we paraded past him. He stood on a simple dais accompanied by three or four senior officers from the other services. All went well as far as the regiment was concerned, we kept station behind RHQ and, standing stiffly to attention, 'eyes righted' as Pat de Clermont raised his arm in salute. There were few civilians to be seen and although the band was playing, we could hear little and the whole affair seemed a bit flat. The 'lift' in parades of this nature comes from the welcome and the enthusiasm shown by the crowd, sadly all that was lacking.

We were now well established in the Officers' Mess and, as always seems to happen, despite the shortages around you, people appear mysteriously with the little things that make such a difference to life. One such item, flowers for the mess, was produced regularly by an elderly woman who became well known to many of us. She was physically unattractive and in her late sixties. One day she was clearly upset about something and was questioned by Frank Turner, a fluent German speaker, as to the trouble. She explained that she had been raped again by a group of Russian soldiers. When he said, 'What do you mean, again?' she told him that she had been raped or gang raped on eleven occasions since the city had fallen. All this by Russian soldiers. Her daughter, who was in her twenties, had been raped as well but 'only twice'. Her daughter had now become a nervous recluse and would neither go out of the apartment nor stand or sit near the window. Her mother was obviously at her wits' end. A few weeks later, a note appeared in the divisional intelligence bulletin that 357 cases of rape by Russians had been reported in the British sector during the first month of our occupation. We were powerless to help during those early days, but as we became more established and active in the sector, so the Russian presence diminished and such excesses became less common.

I was very strict about applying the non-fraternisation ban, having lost my mother recently, and at that stage did not speak to Germans. I had some responsibilities in the Officers' Mess, so I did have to speak to the staff there, who were all very cooperative although slightly servile. I smoked at least twenty cigarettes a day and had to buy more anyway, so I never needed to take part in any black market activity. I served in Germany until January 1950, learned little German – a fact that later I regretted – and during those five years I never had a German girlfriend, which looking back, I also regretted!

There is a wonderful line in Brecht's masterpiece *The Threepenny Opera* which goes 'First food then morals'. Undoubtedly, those who wished to, found themselves kind-hearted girls but managed their affairs with discretion. Two of my friends were involved with two very pretty sisters and they spent happy nights in a flat near Charlottenburg. I asked one of them how they paid for their favours. Apparently they took a couple of bottles of champagne, whatever food they could cadge from the Officers' Mess kitchen, and always left twenty cigarettes. Cheap at the price, I imagine! However, in order to survive, or to obtain food or medical supplies for their families, women resorted to making themselves available, which I felt was a sort of rape and that it was wrong for anyone to take advantage of it. There were some very pretty girls around after the Russians left our zone, there were cases of real love stories developing and, after the non-frat ban was lifted, several British soldiers married Berlin girls.

We were under strict injunction not to become involved in any Russian–German dispute. This became particularly pertinent during one weekend. Bob, Johnny, Douglas Rampf and I were driving back from the city to the Officers' Mess in Bob's jeep. The street was well filled with civilians and we were travelling very slowly down what was essentially a shopping area. As we approached a side turning we became aware that a scuffle was taking place in the middle of the road and we heard a woman scream. Bob stopped the jeep and we saw a German man, shouting 'Dieb, Dieb', chasing a Russian officer up the side street. There was a short burst of sub-machine gun fire and the German fell to the ground. The Russian carried on running and two other Russians who had obviously been covering him, fell in behind him, still menacing the crowd with their guns as they retreated into a doorway and disappeared from view. Meanwhile the unfortunate woman ran up to her husband who was lying in the road. He was dead.

A German policeman materialised and took charge of the situation, which had all happened in a matter of seconds. Apparently the Russian had snatched the woman's handbag. We felt totally mortified that we had been unable to offer any help and although, under the circumstances, it was very unlikely that we could even have influenced the situation, it left us filled with fury and frustration. This was not the sort of event for which our training had prepared us.

Worse however was to follow. One evening Tony Hind, Frank Saxby and I went out to the Officers' Club at Gatow. This was in an attractive building with a garden running down to a huge lake, the Tegensee. Potsdam, where the Conference was being held, was on the far shore. There were of course, clubs for all ranks and this one was staffed by very well trained and very professional German waiters. German champagne cost so little in RM that we drank it like water. That evening we were riding in a 15cwt truck, with the three of us crammed on the front seat, Tony driving. The route to Gatow skirted the Russian Zone near Spandau, where our friends the 11th Hussars were in barracks, and we stopped off there for a drink before driving the last few miles to the club. There was a short piece of open country at one point and as we reached it, we found ourselves driving directly behind a Russian truck with a group of their soldiers standing or sitting in the back. Our headlights were on, although it was not yet really dark, so we dropped back and kept about 75 yards between the two vehicles. Suddenly the Russian truck swung out into the middle of the road, braked sharply and stopped. Tony's reaction was to slam on our brakes too and, thinking there had been an accident, we threw open our doors ready to get out. Meanwhile a Russian soldier leapt out of the back of the truck and then we saw that there was a woman with a bicycle at the roadside. The soldier wrenched the bicycle from the woman's hands, and she was dragged after him as she struggled to hold on to it. Instinctively we all jumped out of the vehicle to help her, but as we did so, there was a sound of a shot, the woman slumped to the ground, the soldier threw the bicycle and himself into the truck which was already on the move, and by the time we had got to her, they were roaring off down the road and practically out of sight in the failing light. She was dead. An elderly frau, harmless, probably going back to her house with some food, killed for a bicycle. Some German civilians appeared, took her body to an adjacent house and reported the matter. We heard no more of it. Life was cheap.

We considered ourselves to be fairly hardened veterans, but killing women was not a part of our philosophy or experience and we were all thoroughly sickened by the event. Obviously stories were exaggerated and were elaborated as they were passed on, but it seemed abundantly clear to us that the Russians had been given carte-blanche to carry out any excess in Berlin as a means of punishing and totally subduing the population. Later in August, a friend told me about a Russian colonel who was commanding one of the Mongolian divisions. He used to attend the parties which were held to try to create a forum of some kind of understanding between the occupying powers. One evening, after a few drinks, he was separated from his political commissar for a minute and said to a divisional officer, 'Don't judge the Russian people by these Mongolian savages – only the Muscovites are civilised,' or words to that effect. He disappeared a few days later, sacked for his indiscretion, or so our intelligence believed.

The soldiers, too, found the Russian behaviour unacceptable and even Alan Howard, who had looked forward to meeting them with such pleasure, was taken aback. He took one look at them on entering the city, was shocked and spent a couple of days polishing his boots and webbing before going out. This in no way indicated any reduction in his socialist principles. I was amused and rather proud too, to hear that when we had mock elections in the regiment, run by the Education Officer as a means of preparing us for the real elections which were to follow, he stood as the Socialist candidate. I can't remember whether he was elected or not.

Life in the Officers' Mess was great fun, rather boisterous and noisy but entertaining. There were other activities in Berlin. On one occasion we went to the opera in the Bismarckstrasse which was interesting, many German fans were there, mostly elderly women dressed up in their furs and hats. There were several night clubs in the Kurfurstendam, which were soon placed off limits. There was a cinema and a NAAFI run club for other ranks called the Blau-Weiss Club. Remarkably, too, there was a very athletic ballet company, Die Wessens; in fact life was astonishingly normal in so many ways, despite the fact that the population were ill fed. Large numbers of them crammed into the train at the weekend to get out into the country to buy or barter for food. I am sure that the farmers did well, as those houses which we entered during the fighting all had cellars full of bottled foods. The train had a lovely German name which I noted, the *nichtverhungenzug*, non-starvation train. A large part of the inhabitants lived in cellars or crowded into rooms, one saw cooking going on in the streets, sanitation was awful but improving, water often came from a communal tap and so on – I imagine that parts of London and Coventry were not dissimilar at some point in the war.

I was writing a great deal of poetry at this time, a sure sign that I was worried by what I was seeing and feeling very confused as to how to respond. My engagement to Audrey was becoming a matter of deep concern to me, my beliefs in justice were being shaken by the situation I saw around me in Berlin, I felt deeply the suffering that I was seeing, and yet powerless to do anything about it. Although I was never a heavy drinker, I certainly drank more as a result of this and, as one of the leading members of a gang of boisterous young men, found that it was easy to play and forget temporarily. One of these poems, which begins with the lines:

Oppressed, downtrodden, spurned by all,
They sweat and labour in the sun

reflects this feeling of suppression of rights and the injustice which followed. Heady stuff for a 21-year-old. Looking back on it all, I suppose that I was ready to be one of Alan Howard's most fervent converts. It was lucky that he could not see my poetry book!

The Potsdam Conference began on Sunday 15 July and, although we were not directly involved in providing the guards of honour or the protective lining of routes and so on we were still very busy preparing for the Victory Parade itself. My Russian speaking troopers were already at Potsdam and we did not see them for a couple of weeks. Even after their return, they were very discreet about making any comments. From such talks as I had with them, however, I gathered the impression that, even at their level, they felt that Messrs Churchill and Truman had been 'conned' by Mr Stalin. It added to their deep concern about the future for 'stateless' people such as them. Incidentally many of us spent the Sunday basking in sunshine at the Gatow Club, enjoying the marvellous views over the promon tory on which the conference was being held.

On 16 July it was announced that Mr Churchill had selected Saturday 21 July as the date for the parade. General relief was expressed all round that it would soon be over and that life could return to normal.

The great day dawned very early indeed, as seems to happen with ceremonial parades, and by 0730hrs, having been up since 0500hrs we were all in position and had been inspected by almost every rank of senior officer. We were the second senior Army unit on parade, following the RHA, and were drawn up in line on either side of the Charlottenburger Chaussee just to the east of the Victory Column. It was a wet morning but the rain had stopped shortly after dawn and the roads dried out quickly. We were wearing battledress with shoulder webbing and pistols. To their chagrin, officers were instructed to wear berets and not the regimental green and gold side hats.

We were allowed to 'fall out' for an hour before the parade started and we stood about by the tanks, smoking and gossiping; it was all very relaxed. Sgt Godwin and I walked down through the Tier Garten to try and get a closer view of the saluting base, but were turned back by military police who were patrolling the approaches. There were a fair number of civilians walking about, but they were prevented from getting too close to the saluting base itself, certainly at our end anyway.

Shortly after 0930hrs we 'stood to' by crews in front of our vehicles, officers at the head of each troop or squadron. We were then told to 'stand at ease' pending inspection. At 1000hrs, the 3rd Royal Horse Artillery, senior Army regiment on parade and 'right of the line', fired a salute. This told us that Mr Churchill and all his distinguished guests had arrived on the saluting base. Shortly afterwards an impeccable half tracked vehicle appeared from my right, in the back of which stood Mr Churchill and Field Marshal Montgomery. There were six other half tracks following, all containing distinguished guests, but as we were standing stiffly to attention at this time, I couldn't register who they were. They completed the tour to our left and then reappeared on the other side of the Charlottenburger Chaussee, reviewing the remainder as they returned to the saluting base.

The order was given to mount and we clambered into our tanks and waited to be told to 'start up'. This was given over the wireless at about 1045hrs and to our profound relief, every vehicle started without demur. It would have been very ignominious to have got this far and then remained sitting there as all the others roared off.

The march past began at 1050hrs, about 20 minutes late,

and we pulled out on to the road, forming into lines as we moved off. The regiment, having been sited near the Victory Column with the saluting base only 200 yards beyond it, did not have far to go. A contingent from the Royal Navy Chatham, as the senior service, had taken their place at the head of the parade. Following them, right of the line, were elements of the 3rd and then the 5th RHA, all very close friends of ours. We were the first regiment to have to circumvent the Column and then line ourselves up again, but we had done this before so it did not present any problem. As we approached the saluting base, I was standing stiffly to attention, eyes glued to Pat de Clermont so as to 'eyes right' as he saluted. We had to retain this position until we had cleared it. Being the leader of the column which was next to the dais itself, I had a very clear view of all those standing there. Mr Churchill stood slightly to the fore, wearing a light coloured service dress and a peaked dress hat. He was standing, looking directly up the Chaussée, and saluted us in answer to the colonel's salute. Standing next to him and a little behind him was Mr Attlee, in civilian clothes and bare headed. Then Field Marshals Alanbrooke and Montgomery with the tall, bare headed figure of Mr Anthony Eden to the left of the Field Marshals; General Lyne was standing to the right of the Prime Minister as we faced him, together with a senior naval officer whom I didn't recognise. I also spotted Mr Morrison, and then it was all over and we were past. At that point all vehicles accelerated slightly as we had to ensure that we dispersed quickly so as not to hold up those who were behind us.

As soon as we reached the tank park, we dismounted and lorries took a number of the longer serving other ranks back to the city to the new 'Winston' Club for ORs which was to be opened formally by Mr Churchill. It was there that he made his marvellous, emotional 'Dear Desert Rats! May your glory ever shine!' speech. Many of those who were there, including my late troop sergeant, Bill Pritchard, were terribly moved by it. Bill, who was standing quite close to Mr Churchill at the time, said that the great man had tears in his eyes as he spoke. Whatever the truth may be, he also took the opportunity of granting a day's holiday and that went down very well with all.

One day when I was at the club, I met the officer who was responsible for the administration of the mail plane which left Berlin nightly for England. I had just received a letter from Audrey to say that she was ill and had to go into the Samaritan hospital for an operation and I told him how much I wanted to get back to see her. 'No problem,' he said, 'Report to me at 1900hrs on Friday.' I asked the adjutant for a weekend's leave and duly reported to Gatow. I was then slipped on to the mail plane, a Dakota, and we took off for England at 2000hrs. I hadn't really thought the matter through and I was dumbfounded when we landed at Lyneham and it was only 2020hrs. I had not realised that there was a two-hour time differential, Berlin being on Central European Time. I returned on the Sunday evening rather dispirited and uncertain as to how to handle my personal problems. My father was in Palestine at this time and I had no one to advise me.

Meanwhile the pleasures of being in Berlin were becoming self- evident. The regiment was now well established and the accommodation excellent. We had restored the Olympic swimming pool to working order and it was bliss to have a swim in the superb weather that we were enjoying.

A regimental sports day was arranged, and I was involved as I had run for Northern Command in 1943 and had run a fast hundred yards, winning that event. The acknowledged speed merchant in the regiment was Sgt Arnold. A lot of money was staked on the race, I believe, and whoever backed me must have lost heavily. Arnold pipped me by a whisker, but I went on to win the 220 yards easily. As a result of this I was one of those chosen to run against a French team. This time I won the 100 yards event but threw away the 220 yards by letting my wily French opponent make me feel that I could win easily. I tried to take him on the closing bend, but he managed to keep me out and then produced a fine finish which left me well behind. A good lesson in tactics.

Life in our own regimental Officers' Mess was very pleasant and we had great fun there. Dinner nights when guests were invited from other regiments were especially enjoyable, but most nights developed into a party of one sort or another. One of our favourite pastimes was to play sardines – sounds very dull until you have experienced being one of half a dozen men balanced on the top of a door, or a windowsill. It was all good clean fun. Tim Pierson, Tony and I had fallen in love with Ingrid Bergman in the classic film *Casablanca*, just released. We saw it three or four times, just in order to relish the scene where, leaning back provocatively against the door post, she asks, in a deep sexy voice, 'Anybody got-a-light?' We did not need much entertaining!

Although we had commandeered most of the houses in our road, there were other residents and almost opposite to the mess itself was a large house containing civilian staff from, I presume, the British government offices in Berlin. To our delight, the most exquisite little Chinese actress lodged in that house, although, unfortunately, no member of our mess managed to get to know her. One night an unmarked, unlit jeep was parked outside and Pat de Clermont ordered it to be towed away as no vehicles were permitted to be left unattended in the street. Later that night, much later, a rather red faced and very angry brigadier appeared demanding the return of his jeep. We did not see him there again!

Some of the officers were selected to go and dine with the Russians in the Eastern Zone. One of these was Geoffrey Gould, now fully recovered from his wounds. He was in our billet and I envied him the chance. However, when he returned at about 0100hrs, I went down to meet him and he seemed to be close to death. His breathing was shallow, he was totally unconscious and it was very frightening. Bill Best and I struggled in with him, he was a large man, while someone else woke up Jimmie our doctor. 'Stomach pump and quick,' was his immediate response and off they went to the hospital. Geoffrey came back a couple of days later, a wiser and somewhat chastened man.

He told me later that when they arrived at the Russian Officers' Mess they were plied with drink, a fierce white vodka he thought. Geoffrey had been warned and tried to dispose of as much as possible, but the toasts were direct and difficult to avoid. By the time they sat down to dinner he felt as if he'd had enough, but during dinner and afterwards the toasts continued. Some of the Russians seemed impervious, but the tempo was fierce and he felt that it was quite normal for them to behave like that. He managed to walk out at the end, but then remembered no more.

Another officer whom I met at the club, and who had attended a similar function, said that he had found himself seated at a table between two German girls. One told him that the Russians went out in the day and if they saw a girl they fancied, took her identity or her ration card and told her to collect it from the barracks that evening. To be without either at this time spelt disaster, so she had to go. The unfortunate girl so chosen then served at table and later carried out any other service required. He found that at his party the officers were so drunk that he was able to pour most of the toasts down the neck of his battledress, and so stayed sober but acted as if he was drunk too. He added that he reckoned that the drink, which ran down his chest and legs, had rotted his shoes as well!

On 15 August, the final peace was signed and the war ended in Japan. VJ Day was marked by a regimental parade and a thanksgiving service. There was relief too that none of us would have to be drafted to the Pacific region to continue the war there.

I had been promoted to Captain earlier in the month and it was pointed out to me that apart from sick leave and a long weekend, I had had no real break since my embarkation leave in 1943. I was reluctant to go as I had no home base to return to, my father still being in Palestine. However, it made sense to use the opportunity; my squadron leader, Johnnie Robertson, agreed, as did Tim Pierson, and I left Berlin by train for England at the end of August. I returned after a week to spend three weeks with what was, from then on, to become my real family, the de Smets of Ghent in Belgium. Just before I left, I was told that by the time I returned, the regiment would have gone back to Itzehoe, in Schleswig-Holstein, so it was 'Goodbye Berlin', for me. I had begun to feel very much at home there and was quite sorry to leave.

As far as I was concerned this was the end of an era. It had been a long journey for me from school, through the military training machine, the Middle East tour, the invasion and subsequent battles. I had undoubtedly matured a great deal and had lost much of my 'schoolboy' image. I owed a great deal to the regiment, their support, their encouragement and their companionship. I was about to be gazetted as a regular officer in the 8th Kings Royal Irish Hussars and they were now very much my family. I could identify with the words of the regimental song, which begins:

> I'm a soldier in the Kings Army,
> I'm a galloping Eighth Hussar,
> I sail the ocean wide and blue
> I'm a chap who knows a thing or two . . .

I looked forward to my future in that family with pleasure and confidence.

Index

Note: Italic page numbers refer to illustrations.